Between the Black Desert and the Red

Between the Black Desert and the Red

Turkmen Carpets from the Wiedersperg Collection

ROBERT PINNER

MURRAY L. EILAND, JR.

FINE ARTS MUSEUMS OF SAN FRANCISCO

Published on the occasion of the exhibition
Between the Black Desert and the Red
Turkmen Carpets from the Wiedersperg Collection

Fine Arts Museums of San Francisco
M. H. de Young Memorial Museum

18 December 1999 to 25 June 2000

Between the Black Desert and the Red: Turkmen Carpets from the Wiedersperg Collection
has been organized by the Fine Arts Museums of San Francisco.

Published with the assistance of the Andrew W. Mellon Foundation Endowment
for Publications and with additional help from Gisela and Wolfgang Wiedersperg.

First published in the United States of America in softcover in 1999 by the Fine Arts
Museums of San Francisco. Distributed by Antique Collectors' Club, Ltd., New York.
Market Street Industrial Park, Wappingers Falls, NY 12590, phone 914-297-0003.

Library of Congress Catalog Card Number 99-63902

ISBN 0-88401-099-6

Printed and bound in Belgium.

Front Cover: Beshir carpet (detail), pl. 70
Frontispiece: Salor trapping (detail), pl. 4
Page 10: Karakalpak or Uzbek carpet (detail), pl. 78
Page 116: Yomut main carpet (detail), pl. 38
Page 124: Tekke rug (detail), pl. 14
Page 136: Beshir carpet (detail), pl. 74

Contents

Foreword

This book and the exhibition it accompanies celebrate an important collection of Turkmen carpets and textiles donated to the Fine Arts Museums of San Francisco in 1997 by San Francisco residents Wolfgang and Gisela Wiedersperg. Like many other collectors, the Wiederspergs, who settled in the Bay Area in 1956, purchased their first carpets to furnish their home. When they found that filling their floors and walls had merely whetted their appetites for Turkmen textiles, they embarked on an odyssey of collecting, study, and connoisseurship that lasted more than three decades. The Wiederspergs aimed to create a cross-section of the Turkmen weaving tradition by acquiring the earliest and best pieces they could find. And indeed, the eighty-two Turkmen bags, tent bands, main carpets, door carpets, and decorative hangings given to the Museums include outstanding examples from each of the major rug-weaving tribes—the Arabatchi, Chodor, Ersari, Salor, Saryk, Tekke, and Yomut.

The Wiedersperg collection is the second major gift of Turkmen carpets to come to the Museums in a decade. The gift of this collection is a vital opportunity to enhance understanding of a significant weaving culture. Our delight in the collection and gratitude for the Wiederspergs' generosity is tempered only by the sadness that Mr. Wiedersperg did not live to see the completion of this project. Thanks to his generosity and that of his wife, and to the earlier patronage of Caroline and H. McCoy Jones, as well as the recently promised gifts from George and Marie Hecksher, the Fine Arts Museums have become arguably the most important repository of high quality, non-classical carpets in the United States.

An exhibition and major catalogue inevitably demand the participation of many people both inside and outside the Museums. We owe thanks to Bill White and his entire technical production staff, including lighting designer William Huggins; to conservation staff members Sarah Gates, Joanne Hackett, Barbara Nitzberg, Yadin Larochette, and the conservation laboratory volunteers. Special thanks also go to David Walker, Talisman, for his generous help with conservation. Within the Museums other assistance was provided by Kathe Hodgson, director of exhibitions planning; by development staff members Barbara Boucke and Anne-Marie Bonfilio; and by media relations staff members Pamela Forbes, Barbara Traisman, and Andrew Fox. The catalogue could not have been produced without Ann Heath Karlstrom and Karen Kevorkian of the publications department, some timely help from Juliana Pennington of design, as well as the invaluable outside support of copy editor Frances Bowles, designer Christine Taylor, and photographer Don Tuttle and his assistant Joe James. We are also grateful to James Blackmon, for his efforts to bring the collection to the Museums, and to a number of other contributors, including other lenders of photographic material—Kate FitzGibbon and Andrew Hale; Sotheby's, New York; the American Foundation for Textile Arts, Inc.; and the Metropolitan Museum of Art—and to George Hecksher, Bea Weicker Irvin, Marla Mallett, Kurt Munkacsi, Michael Rotherberg, and John Sommer for their comments and suggestions. Diane Mott, associate curator of textiles, ably curated the exhibition as well as vigorously shepherded the catalogue to completion, with support from curator Melissa Leventon and Jennifer Minniti. Finally, our thanks to Robert Pinner and Murray L. Eiland, Jr., for their splendid catalogue essay.

Harry S. Parker III
Director of Museums

Between the Black Desert and the Red

The Wiedersperg Collection
of Turkmen Rugs

Described as the chamber music of the repertoire, Turkmen weavings have been collected by museums and individuals since at least the second half of the nineteenth century. Possibly because of their rich variety, more Turkmen weavings are to be found in collections in the United States and Germany (the two countries with the largest number of private rug collections) than are weavings of other provenance. Turkmen knotted-pile textiles and to a lesser extent flatweaves include carpets in numerous sizes and many different shapes, rug-shaped tent-door hangings, bags, trappings, bands, and other objects woven, like rugs, in knotted pile. Weavings from other areas in the region tend to show less variety in both form and function. In the past three decades a great interest in these weavings has developed and has resulted, not only in a burgeoning literature on the subject, but also in a vastly improved recognition of just who the Turkmen are and what their rugs are all about. Among the major collections generated by this interest, that assembled by Wolfgang and Gisela Wiedersperg of San Francisco is recognized as being among the world's finest and most comprehensive. Some of the Wiedersperg rugs have appeared in publications throughout the word as the most exquisite examples of their particular types.

To like Turkmen rugs, one must like the color red. There are a few white-ground pieces, but the predominant color of most early Turkmen rugs is madder red, which may vary from a brick red to a dark purple brown. Early Turkish rugs are similar in this respect, but in relatively fewer Persian and Caucasian tribal and village rugs is the color red as extensively and consistently dominant. The prevailing red ground indicates the sense of continuity of the Turkmen weaving tradition, as does the endless pattern repeat format, which is the basis of almost all Turkmen field designs—the field being the major central panel, which is usually framed by one or more border stripes.

The origins of the Turkmen people are controversial, but during the past millennium, Turkmen have constituted a recognized ethnic group in Central Asia and, in particular, in the area east of the Caspian Sea, extending eastward to the Amu Darya and south into what is now northern Iran and Afghanistan (see map). Living both as farmers, where there is enough water, and as pastoral nomads in the drier regions, the Turkmen are likely to have woven rugs all of this time although most of the rugs in modern collections were probably made in the past two hundred years. In much of the earlier literature on these rugs, the word Turkoman has been used, but there is little reason for continuing a tradition that falls short of our best current understanding. The largest population of these people is to be found in Turkmenistan, which became a sovereign nation when the Soviet Union dissolved. The people there clearly call themselves Turkmen, a word of two syllables rather than three. Having recently adopted the Turkish alphabet for their language, they are, strictly speaking, Türkmen.

Turkmen rugs are made by separate but related groups of weavers that we describe as tribes and subtribes, each of which has traditionally woven rugs for the same general purposes: carpets, called main carpets (for the floor of the felt tent, or *yurt,* in which the nomadic Turkmen lived); hangings to cover doorways; bags of different types and sizes for storage and transport; and various decorative trappings used mainly in the rituals of the Turkmen wedding.

Throughout the region where rugs are woven, names are assigned according to varying criteria. Rugs from Iran (often described as Persian rugs) are usually identified by a place-name, that of the city, town, or district in which they were woven. Rugs from rural areas inhabited by various tribal groups such as the Qashqa'i, Baluchi, or Kurds are usually named after the tribe. Rugs from Turkey are also usually identified by place-names, those of the region, town, or cluster of villages where the weavings tend to be of the same type. Less frequently they are named for the various nomadic or seminomadic groups who do the weaving. Rugs made by the Turkmen tribes of Central Asia are, however, seldom identified by place-names because the various tribes tended to move as the local balance of power shifted. To use a place-name such as the Merv Oasis to label a rug would give no indication of which of the three main tribal alliances that have successively lived in that area for the past century and a half might have made the rug. For Turkmen rugs, a tribal name is most useful, provided that it is based on solid information rather than

Regions Inhabited by Turkmen During the Nineteenth Century

KAZAKHSTAN

Mangishlak Peninsula

Aral Sea

Syr Darya

Kizil Kum Desert (Red Sands)

KYRGYZSTAN

Tashkent

Porsu • Nukus
Konya Urgench •
Tashauz • • Urgench
Khiva

Amu Darya

UZBEKISTAN

Bukhara • Samarkand •

TAJIKISTAN

Caspian Sea

Türkmenbashy (Krasnovodsk)
• Cheleken

Kara Kum Desert (Black Sands)

TURKMENISTAN

Denau •
Chardjou

Karshi •

Dushanbe

Balkhan Mtns.

Kizil Atrek

Geok-Tepe •
Ashkhabad

Merv Oasis

Burdalyk

Kerki •

Kopet-Dagh Mtns.
Gorgan *Atrek*

Tejend •
Yuletan •

Murghab

Andkhui •
• Shibergan

Gorgan (Astrabad) •

Sarakhs •

Mashhad •

Pende •

• Maimana

Tehran

Kabul

IRAN

Herat •

AFGHANISTAN

LEGEND
★ Capital
• City or Town
~ River
— Current National Boundary
▢ Deserts (Red and Black Sands)
▲ Mountains

PLACE NAMES. The names of places in the Central Asian Republics of the former Soviet Union appear in rug literature and elsewhere spelled in ways that are bewilderingly inconsistent. Given the history of the region, it is no wonder. Turkmen was written in a modified Arabic alphabet until the Russian conquest, when cyrillic supplanted it. Neither was particularly well suited to the accurate representation of the sound system of the Turkmen language, and both gave rise to a number of transliterations. With the dis-

solution of the U.S.S.R., Turkmenistan began converting to the Latin alphabet, which it is adapting to the Turkmen language. As a result, spellings are very much in flux. The most widely used of the older transliterations, which are used above and elsewhere in this book, appear below on the left, with their most current equivalents on the right.

Andkhui	Andkhvoy
Ashkabad	Ashgabat
Astrabad, Astarabad	Gorgan
Bukhara	Bukhoro
Chardzhou, Chardjou	Chärjew
Charshango	Charshanga
Denau	Deynau
Geok-Tepe	Gökdepe
Kara Kum, Karakum	Garagum

Karshi	Qarshi
Khiva	Khiwa
Kizil Atrek	Gyzyletrek
Kizil Kum, Kizilkum	Qizilqum
Konya Urgench	Köneürgench
Kopet-Dagh	Köpetdagershi
Krasnovodsk	Türkmenbashy
Maimana	Meymaneh
Mangishlak	Mangyshlak
Mari	Mary
Murghab	Murgab
Porsu	Porsy
Samarkand	Samarqand
Tashauz	Dashowuz
Tashkent	Toshkent
Tejend	Tejen
Urgench	Urganch
Yuletan, Yoletan	Yolöten

Inset map labels: BYELARUS, RUSSIA, UKRAINE, KAZAKHSTAN, ROMANIA, Caspian Sea, Aral Sea, Black Sea, GREECE, TURKEY, UZBEKISTAN, KYRGYZSTAN, CHINA, Mediterranean Sea, SYRIA, LEBANON, ISRAEL, IRAQ, TURKMENISTAN, TAJIKISTAN, JORDAN, KUWAIT, IRAN, AFGHANISTAN, PAKISTAN, EGYPT, SAUDI ARABIA, Persian Gulf, OMAN, Indian Ocean, INDIA, SUDAN, Red Sea, YEMEN

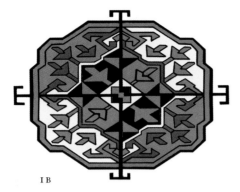

IB

IA

IC

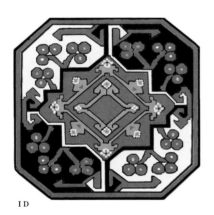

ID

FIG. I. *Gülli (gushly) göls*

A *Gülli (gushly) göl:* Salor, on main carpets

B *Gülli (gushly) göl:* Tekke, on main carpets

C *Gülli (gushly) göl:* Ersari, lobed, on main carpets

D *Gülli (gushly) göl:* Ersari, straight-sided, on main carpets

speculation. The principal tribal groups to whom rug weaving has been attributed during the past two hundred years include the Salor, Saryk, Tekke, Yomut, Ersari, Kizil Ayak, Chub Bash, Chodor, and Arabachi. Of the other tribes that frequent the region, some probably wove rugs, others did not. An exception to this convention of naming rugs for their weavers is the Beshir rug (see pl. 70). Made in towns and villages on both sides of the middle reaches of the Amu Darya, the type is named after a town in the region and the rugs were apparently woven by a local population belonging to the Ersari or Salor and even by people who were not Turkmen. When rugs are attributed to a tribal group which cannot be identified by name, it may be labeled by a design motif, e.g., the so-called "eagle" gul rugs. In another system of labeling, certain Turkmen rugs are classified by the design motif known as the eagle *gul,* described below.

The various types of woven articles have names that are generally accepted, but not immutable. The names may apply to various forms of the articles and may have different meanings in different parts of the region. Storage bags are often decorated with a pileweave surface or face. Large rectangular bags are usually referred to as *chuvals* (see pl. 2), but other Western spellings such as *juval* are also in use. The bags may have an additional broad band, an *alem* (or *elem),* woven below the field and decorated with different designs or—as in many Yomut chuvals—left bare. Turkmen bags generally open on a long side. Similar bags of the same name are used in Turkey, most of those opening on one of the short sides. The *torba* is a smaller, shallower bag (see pl. 23), which usually does not have an alem below the field. The smallest bags are called *kaps* or *mafrash*s (see pl. 43). The pile-weave hangings used to cover tent doorways (see pl. 7) are called *ensi*s and these differ in size and design from one tribe to another. The trappings are named according to their purpose, *asmalyk*s being wedding trappings that are usually five-sided (see pl. 26).

The most common decorative motif in Turkmen carpets is a roughly octagonal, at times rather flattened or lobed ornament

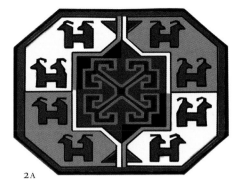
2A

2B

(known generically as a *gul*) that is often quartered and usually placed in rows in an endless repeat design. Usually, but not always, the design is varied with alternating rows of a second, minor ornament. The meaning of the word *gül* is not in doubt. In Persian and Turkmen it stands for "flower"; in Turkish, more specifically, for "rose." In the terminology of Western art history, the device is called a "rosette." To some degree, the sources of repeat designs incorporating *guls* are generally accepted as being the roundels and intermediate motifs used in the silk fabrics made by the Sasanians, Sogdians, Byzantines, and Chinese.[1] In this catalogue we distinguish between the primary and secondary ornaments of most carpets as *göls* and *güls* respectively, and use the simpler spelling, *gul,* when referring to the device in a generic sense as, for instance, in differentiating gul rugs from those with other designs. The distinction between *göl* and *gül* was first proposed in 1946 by V. G. Moshkova, a pioneer of fieldwork among the Turkmen,[2] and has been adopted in much of the literature.

Göls are found in numerous variant forms, some used by only a few weavers, others found in the work of several different tribes. Three of the major carpet-weaving Turkmen tribes, the Tekke, Salor, and Ersari, and some of the weavers of the Saryk have decorated their main carpets (but not other weavings) with the ornament called the *gülli* or *gushly göl,* the names being derived from the Turkmen: *gülli göl* meaning "flower" *göl*; *gushly* from *gush* or *kush,* meaning "bird" (see figs. 1A–D and pl. 1). Weavers from five other tribes—the Arabachi, Chodor, and some groups of the Yomut and Ersari, including the Kizil Ayak—have used a type known as the *tauk nuska göl* (see figs. 2A–C and pl. 53).[3] In fact, both of these major *göls* include symbols that are interpreted as birds, or parts of birds, by the Turkmen. Both have also been used by other Central Asian weavers, particularly by the Uzbek. The Arabachi also use a distinctive form of *gushly* gul on chuvals. Other Uzbeks and perhaps some Karakalpak weavers have used versions of the *tauk nuska göl.* A related *göl,* used on main carpets by the Saryk and Ersari, is the *omurga* or *temirjin göl* (see fig. 3 and pl. 5).

2C

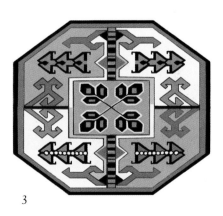
3

FIG. 2. *Tauk nuska göls*
A *Tauk nuska göl:* on main carpet of several Turkmen tribes including the Yomut, Arabachi, Chodor, Kizil Ayak, and Ersari groups
B *Tauk nuska göl:* on Karakalpak and Uzbek carpets
C *Tauk nuska göl:* on Karakalpak and Uzbek carpets

FIG. 3. *Omurga (temirjin) göl*

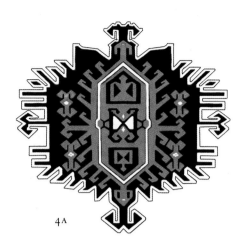

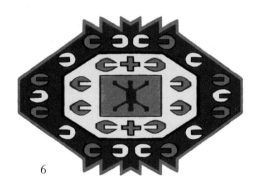

4A

4B

5

6

7

8

FIG. 4. Eagle guls
A Group III
B Group II

FIG. 5. *Kepse (kapza)* gul

FIG. 6. "C" gul

FIG. 7. *Dyrnak göl*

FIG. 8. Serrated rosette gul

At least two, and possibly three, groups of rugs are distinguished by the eagle gul and are named after this design feature (see figs. 4A–B and pls. 28 and 29). The rugs are the work of weavers whose tribes have not yet been conclusively identified. The name is also used for rugs that are known to belong to the same group because of their structure and colors, but that have different designs. Among the other major ornaments to be found on main carpets are three guls used predominantly by Yomut groups: the *kepse* (or *kapza*) gul (see fig. 5 and pl. 33), the "C" gul (see fig. 6 and pl. 31), and the *dyrnak göl* (see fig. 7 and pl. 34). Another Yomut gul, the "serrated rosette" gul, appears only rarely (see fig. 8 and pl. 32). In many Yomut carpets the *dyrnak göl* (a hooked diamond ornament ubiquitous in Central Asia and different parts of Iran and Turkey) is used in both major (*göl*) and minor (*gül*) forms in the same piece (as in pl. 34); in eagle gul carpets it is used only as a secondary device (see pl. 28).

Perhaps inevitably there has been speculation about the totemic character of the Turkmen *göl,* a thesis that Moshkova suggested first, along with a hypothesis about "live" and "dead" göls.[4] While there is little evidence that Turkmen *göls* had a totemic function, that is not to deny that they are heraldic in character. Indeed, when a single ornament is used over a long period by one tribe and or a group of tribes, it could hardly avoid acquiring such a status. On this subject one might make several observations.

- Invariably, the main carpets of some of the carpet-weaving tribes, such as the Tekke, Salor, Arabachi, and possibly the major tribal Ersari groups, carry the main carpet *göl* associated with the tribe. Other tribes use a variety of *göls*—among them, the Chodor, who use the *ertmen göl* (see fig. 9 and pl. 50) and the *tauk nuska göl*; the Saryk, who use two different forms of *gushly göls* (see figs. 1A–D), the *omurga (temirjin) göl* (see fig. 3), and chuval *guls* on tent bags (see fig. 10 and pl. 3); and the Yomut and smaller tribes that merged with them. For these tribes, it is possible to speculate that the differences in the gul form represent different groups. It is difficult to find any other carpet-weaving entity—tribal, domestic, or workshop—where a single design composition, especially one of primary and secondary ornaments as lobed or straight-sided octagons, is used frequently without the development of significant variations.

- There are usually several options for other ornaments on main carpets. Most Tekke main carpets have one of three secondary ornaments, each of which may be drawn in different forms; one of two designs of border octagons; several different intermediate border ornaments (or none at all); and several minor borders. Similar variation can be found in other tribal carpets.

9

10

FIG. 9. *Ertmen göl:* Chodor

FIG. 10. *Chuval* gul: on some main carpets of the Saryk and Yomut

· There is even more variation in designs on other Turkmen weavings, in the ensis, chuvals and other tent bags, and the asmalyks and other trappings and furnishings woven for weddings.

· A subsidiary argument, which may demonstrate the importance of the major *göl,* is that in most main carpets it is woven entire and, when the field is cut by a border, the cut almost invariably runs through the secondary ornaments.

· The transformation of a design element into a heraldic symbol does not apply to all individual tribes or all carpet *göls.* On the one hand, the *tauk nuska göls* on carpets made by different tribes are often drawn with similar internal ornamentation and are difficult to distinguish from one another. In this case it is possible to assume that the *göl* belongs to a federation of tribes. On the other hand, different Yomut groups use several ornaments on their main carpets, such as the *kepse* gul, the "C" gul, and the eagle gul, that lack the quartered form. These, and some other guls that are used without secondary ornaments, may have developed outside the Turkmen tradition and be derived from Persian and Caucasian carpet ornaments. A special case may be the *dyrnak* ornament, which in older Yomut carpets is most often shown in a complex *göl* form (with flower or anchorlike motifs) alternating in rows with simpler, and sometimes smaller, *güls* (see pl. 34).

FLATWEAVES

It is for their pile rugs that the Turkmen have become famous; their flatwoven artifacts (rugs without a pile) have been ignored. Many of the small flatwoven twentieth-century covers and tent bags—which reach the market from the Tekke, the Yomut of northern Iran, and from the Ersari and other Turkmen tribes in Afghanistan—tend to be monochrome copies of earlier knotted pile rugs and inherently less interesting. But their larger, brocaded weavings, known as *palas,* are neglected unjustifiably. Finely made, and with complex multilevel designs, flatwoven rugs such as those illustrated in plates 79 and 80 are artistically successful.

Neglect by the market has gone in parallel with neglect by scholars. Differences in structural features and colors, which are of primary importance in the taxonomy of Turkmen pileweaves, have hardly been studied in flatweaves, and fieldwork on recent products has been used only for the tentative tribal attribution of older pieces. In Central Asia, Anatolia, and other weaving areas tribes who have given up weaving knotted pile often continue to produce the same kinds of objects using flatweave techniques. The reasons may be complex and varied, but in general, flatweaves are made in less time and with a poorer quality materials.

Turkmen rugs have been collected most avidly during the past thirty years, and several theories about dating them have surfaced and subsequently been submerged during that time. There was a period in the first half of this century when rugs that were presumed to be older than the standard Turkmen pieces, and whose drawing looked a little more archaic, were often attributed to the eighteenth century. Such dating was particularly inconclusive because for many years we had no early specimens of Turkmen rugs with inscribed dates, no early paintings with Turkmen rugs in them, and only one inventory (that of a Russian palace collection in which a Chodor was listed) that convincingly dates a Turkmen rug before the nineteenth century. Thereafter, an understanding began to grow that most of the standard Turkmen fare—the late Tekke main carpets and ensis, the thick, coarsely knotted Afghans, and others—were commercial products made in the late nineteenth or early twentieth centuries. Some scholars have held until quite recently that there is no convincing reason to date even an early Turkmen rug earlier than the nineteenth century.

Dye analysis has helped clarify several problems about nineteenth- and twentieth-century rugs. For rugs that contain synthetic dyestuffs, the maximum age is known from the date that the dyestuff was first manufactured or introduced into the region. For Turkmen rugs this information is particularly useful in dating examples woven in or after the last quarter of the nineteenth century, a period when azo dyes began to be used widely, and before the 1930s, when azo dyes were largely replaced by a later generation of dyestuffs that were more light and water fast. For some types of Turkmen rugs, the introduction of azo dyes followed quite closely changes in design and color. We find, for example, a proliferation of border stripes and increased used of cochineal red in Tekke products and a darkening of the red ground color toward purple in some Saryk weavings. Thus it is possible to date, with a fair degree of certainty, Turkmen rugs woven after about 1880 and, with progressively less accuracy, rugs woven in the third quarter and back to the middle of the nineteenth century.

During the past few decades several rugs that look as if they are especially early examples have come to light. On visual inspection alone, they appear to be more archaic than most nineteenth-century Turkmen rugs. The rug that was donated to the Metropolitan Museum of Art by James Ballard would be difficult to place in the same century as a typical Yomut main carpet,[5] and a rug owned by George and Marie Hecksher and exhibited at the International Conference on Oriental Rugs in Philadelphia in 1996 shows a combination of archaic forms that seem intermediate between Caucasian- and Persian-style palmettes and Turkmen *guls*.[6] One could scarcely imagine that

Yomut Main Carpet
Early nineteenth century
7 ft. 10 in. × 4 ft. 7 in. (239 × 140 cm)
Wool and goat hair; symmetrical knot,
91 per sq. in.
The Metropolitan Museum of Art,
James F. Ballard Collection,
Gift of James F. Ballard, 1922
22.100.44

Yomut Main Carpet
Eighteenth century
Wool; asymmetrical knot open to the left
5 ft. 5 in. × 7 ft. 4 in. (165 × 223 cm)
George and Marie Hecksher Collection

such rugs do not predate the more typical examples. Among bags and trappings too, several have been cited as being older in appearance, although the criteria for such citations are often subjective. However, while the authors know of many purported datings that have been entirely implausible, not all can be summarily rejected.

Carbon-14 dating may prove more reliable, but for carpets at least, the techniques need to be refined. The scientific basis of the process is scarcely open to question, and organic artifacts several thousands of years old have been dated reasonably precisely. The process was thought to be inaccurate for materials originating in the past three hundred years. Because by far the greatest number of Turkmen rugs date from the past two centuries, the value of the carbon-14 process was discounted. Nonetheless, in a research program recently conducted with the cooperation of the radio-carbon laboratory in Zurich, Switzerland, of fifty apparently early Turkmen rugs that were tested, the results for several indicated that they had been made in the fifteenth or sixteenth century or between the mid-fifteenth and mid-seventeenth centuries.[7] In the future, such findings may result in a body of reliably dated early Turkmen rugs that will help us understand the development of design and the way in which these pieces have evolved in the past four or five hundred years.

Antiquity invariably increases value, but for most of us, the appeal of Turkmen weavings lies rather in their beauty. Their metaphorical likeness to music might not be as mysterious as it would seem. In both there is, perhaps, a similarity of emphasis on rhythmic patterns of opposing motifs and colors and a characteristic integration of continuity and interlocking reciprocal detail on several levels of statement and counterpoint.

The Salor

Long considered among the oldest of the Turkmen tribes, the Salors' history is thought to trace back to the twelfth century and the Salghurids, named as one of the Atabeg dynasties in Fars (1148–1287),[8] but the connection between the Salghurids and the modern Salors has not been conclusively established. Salor-Qazan is, however, the name of one of the heroic characters in the Turkmen epic of Dede Korkut.[9] The Salor tribe was mentioned by Mahmut Kashgari in his thirteenth-century list of the twenty-four Turkmen tribes, and the name Salor (Salghur or Salur) was applied to a Turkmen chieftain, as well as to the tribe, in many legends throughout the next three centuries.

In Barthold's summary of the compendium of Turkmen traditions collected in the seventeenth century by Abul Ghazi, the Salor were considered an ancestral tribe from which other tribes had descended. In his accounts of tribal movements in the sixteenth century, Barthold mentions that parts of the Salor tribe migrated to Mangyshlak while considerable numbers, "ten thousand tents," entered Khorasan and from there migrated to Iraq and Fars.[10] Abul Ghazi also expands on the division of the tribe into the Inner and Outer Salor, which had been mentioned by Jani-Mahmud Khwarazmi in the sixteenth century.[11] This division refers to the Turkmen in Mangyshlak, but appears to have existed also among the Salor in the south of Turkmenistan, where the Inner Salor (those from Khorasan) lived to the west of the Outer Salor to whom were said to belong the Tekke, Saryk, and Yomut. In the late sixteenth century the Salor were part of a federation that included the Okhlu, Göklen, Eymur, and others[12] in the Astrabad region. Abul Ghazi's account of the tribute in sheep that the Turkmen tribes had been forced to pay during the time of his grandfather has been taken as a measure of their numerical strength in the early seventeenth century. The Salor and Ersari were assessed sixteen thousand sheep each and the outer Salor (Tekke, Saryk, and Yomut), eight thousand sheep. Elsewhere the tribute paid by the Hasan-eli (which included the Chodor and Igdir) and the Göklen is given as twelve thousand sheep each and by the Arabachi as four thousand.

Even in the nineteenth century, the Salor, or any other Turkmen tribal entity, were not a single tribe located in one region. Together with the Tekke, they captured Merv in 1843 from the Khivans and fought against the Yomut in Tejend, and at the end of Shah Muhammed's reign in Khorasan they, together with Tekke, Yomut, Göklen, and Saryk, joined Muhammad-Hasan-Khan in a revolt in Sarakhs.[13] Although the presence of parts of the Salor tribe has been reported in the second half of the nineteenth and twentieth centuries in the Amu Darya valley, Uzbekistan, northwest China, and elsewhere, the region of Sarakhs remained the main location for Salor rug weaving during this period.

Salor knotted-pile weavings are generally finely woven with high-quality wool in knot counts slightly below those of the equivalent Tekke rugs. They are woven in the asymmetrical knot, which, in most Salor rugs, is open on the left, but in a substantial minority is open on the right. Attempts to correlate the direction of the knot with the age of a rug has proved controversial. The ground color is madder, but wool dyed with an insect red, cochineal or lac, is frequently found in small areas, such as the interior of guls.

SALOR MAIN CARPETS

The main carpets of the Salor went unrecognized in the West before World War II, the few examples in the literature being attributed to other tribes, while carpets decorated with the so-called Salor (also Mary or Mari) gul (see fig. 11), produced in the main by Tekke

FIG. 11. The Salor gul; also known as the Mary (or Mari) gul, named after Mary, the largest city on the Merv Oasis, built near the ruins of the ancient city of Merv

PLATE 1. Salor main carpet

weavers in Merv Oasis, were misattributed to the Salor. In 1973, when Jon Thompson published his translation, as *Carpets of Central Asia,* of Bogolyubov's work that had originally been published in 1908 in Saint Petersburg, Salor carpets came into their own, being recognized then, in Europe and America, as a distinctive type.[14] Although little is known about the production, their size, as well as their quality and uniformity of weave, suggest that most Salor main carpets were woven in workshops and for use in houses rather than tents.[15]

Plate 1 is a beautiful example of the type. Larger than most other Salor carpets and, indeed, other Turkmen main carpets, it has six rows of thirteen *göls* alternating with rows of small, almost diamond-shaped, secondary *güls.* Although they differ in size and format, Salor main carpets show little variation in design, all known examples having the same primary *göls* and border design and all but one, the same secondary *güls.* Unusually this carpet has retained its plain weave (*kilim*) ends.

TWO SALOR CHUVALS

Salor chuvals of two designs are known. The first, of which the chuval illustrated as plate 2 is an example, has a central row of the ornaments that in the West have become known as the Salor gul and rows of the same ornaments cut by the borders at top and bottom.

PLATE 2. Salor bag *(chuval)*

The secondary gul, a diamond figure constructed of star-filled rectangles, is used on most such chuvals,[16] but the designs of the border and the alems (diagonal rows of small flowers in this chuval) can vary.

The second Salor chuval design, like that of most Turkmen chuvals, is based on guls and is illustrated in plate 3. As in the Salor gul chuval, the design is drawn as an endless repeat, with secondary guls at top and bottom cut by the border. The guls on Turkmen chuvals are usually specific to this type of bag, and differ not only from the main carpet ornaments but also from guls on torbas. Guls on Turkmen chuvals are, however, frequently of the same type as those on kaps from the same tribe. On this bag, the secondary *gül* is that used on Salor main carpets and the border has the *kochanak* design, which is used, sometimes in simplified forms, by weavers of most Turkmen tribes.[17] The alem has a design of stylized trees.

A SALOR TRAPPING

The first published Salor trappings with the *kejebe* design were attributed to the Tekke.[18] In 1969 when Ulrich Schürmann published a trapping that later passed into the Wiedersperg Collection (see pl. 4), he assigned it correctly to the Salor.[19] Trappings of this type were used to decorate the Turkmen bride's camel for the wedding caravan[20] and were woven by the Salor using the kejebe design[21] with three, two, or one *darvaza* gul. The design is also used on trappings by the Chodor, Arabachi, and Ersari. A small version of the design, on a weaving approximately the size of a torba and without the *darvaza* gul, was made by the Salor and particularly by the Saryk, who in the late nineteenth century, produced them in numbers, which suggests that they were made for the market. In spite of missing part of the border at both sides,[22] this trapping is one of the largest known and one of the most beautiful. A kochanak border surrounds the field and the wide alem consists of border stripes with diamond patterns of different sizes.

The Saryk

The first mention of the Saryk appears to be in Abul Ghazi's account in which they, together with the Tekke, are described as descended from the Salor chief Toy Tutmaz and, with the Yomut, comprised the Outer Salor. During the eighteenth and early nineteenth centuries the Saryk, Salor, and Ersari were neighbors in the region of the Amu Darya. According to Wood,[23] the Saryk were probably nomads in the region between Khiva, along the middle Amu Darya, and Merv, occupying Merv in the late eighteenth or early nineteenth century. Part of the tribe remained pastoralists until the end of the nineteenth century, longer than any other Turkmen tribe. Apart from references to small numbers of Saryk mercenaries employed by government officials, the early historical sources have little to say about the Saryk until

PLATE 3 (ABOVE). Salor bag *(chuval)*

PLATE 4 (BELOW). Salor trapping

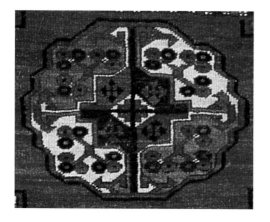

12

13

FIG. 12. Detail of a Saryk carpet with a Salor-like *gülli göl*

FIG. 13. Detail of a Saryk carpet with an Ersari-like *gülli göl*

the 1850s, when the Tekke fought them in Merv and succeeded in evicting them from the region in 1859. During the next decade, the Saryk replaced the Ersari and Salor at Panjdeh,[24] and it is there and at Yuletan that the majority of the Saryk survived during the early days of the Russian occupation.

Except for ensis and torba-sized kejebe-design trappings that were presumably produced for the market in the late nineteenth and early twentieth centuries, Saryk carpets are considerably rarer than those of most other Turkmen tribes. Nevertheless, distinctively different Saryk rugs have sometimes been assigned to various periods or tribal locations. With rare exceptions early Saryk rugs produced in Turkmenistan were woven in the symmetrical knot with a characteristic slightly brownish red field. Most are finely woven with knot counts only slightly lower than those of corresponding Tekke weavings, and most of the white pile is in cotton. A small minority of mainly early rugs has a coarser weave, with ivory wool instead of cotton, and with ornaments more closely related to Ersari products. Saryk bags from the second half of the nineteenth century often have large areas of silk. In late Saryk weavings from the end of the nineteenth century and beginning of the twentieth century, the ground color tends toward a distinctive purple brown or brown.

SARYK MAIN CARPETS

In spite of the rarity of early Saryk main carpets, four different guls are known from surviving examples. The carpets in the Wiedersperg Collection represent the two most frequently encountered. Others are decorated with two different *gushly göls,* one of which (see fig. 12) is similar to the Salor main carpet *göl*, with the animals in the quarters replaced by geometric motifs; the other (see fig. 13) is similar to the Ersari *gülli göl*.

Saryk carpets with the *omurga göl* (also called *temirjin göl*) are rare,[25] and the Wiedersperg example (pl. 5) is one of the most beautiful of its kind. The *göl* resembles the *tauk nuska göl*, but instead of

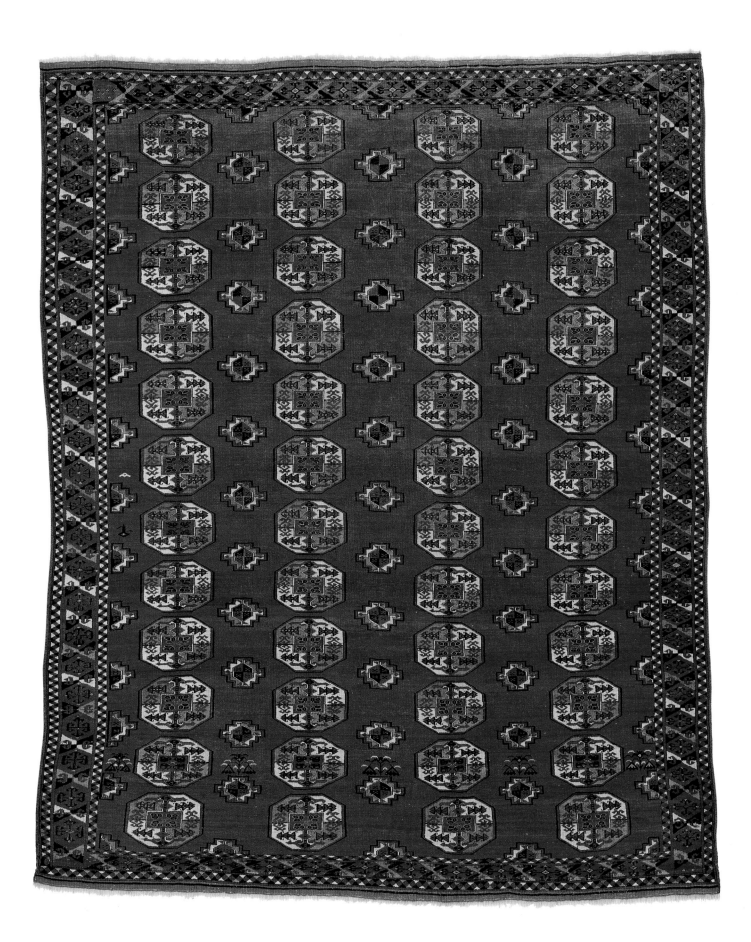

PLATE 5. Saryk main carpet

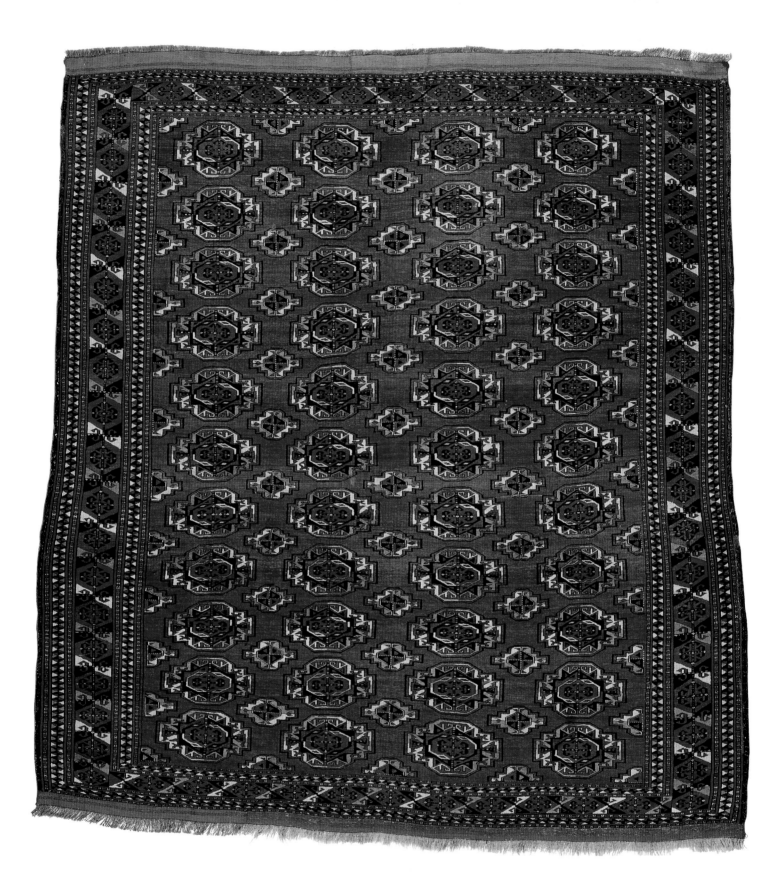

PLATE 6. Saryk main carpet

two-headed birds it shows horizontally connected arrow shapes in the *göl* quarters, a motif also found in some Beshir bags and in Turkish, Caucasian, and Persian tribal rugs. The Ersari, too, particularly those in Afghanistan, use the *omurga göl* on some main carpets, and the relationship between the two tribes is emphasized by shared ornaments, such as a cross with four trefoils, or by a "fleur-de-lis" in the center of the *göl* (to be seen also in the central panel of the ensi in plate 7). This is also a characteristic Ersari motif, which appears in carpets with the *gülli göl*,[26] as is the *naldag* (*nal* is Turkish for "horseshoe" and *dag* means "brand" or "mark") found on the borders of Saryk and Ersari main carpets. An interesting addition to the design is the single line of floral ornaments near the base of the carpet.

The secondary *gül*, a version of the chuval gul, has a role similar to that of the secondary *gül* in Salor carpets (see pl. 1). In some *omurga göl* carpets this motif is replaced by the hooked Memling gul.[27] The design features and color shades that Saryk carpets from this period share with Ersari and Salor carpets support the view that the tribes shared the same territory in the Amu Darya region in the east of Turkmenistan.

A small number of early Saryk carpets and a larger number woven after the mid-nineteenth century are decorated with the Saryk version of the chuval gul. Judging by the ground color and the drawing, the carpet in plate 6 is probably from the mid-nineteenth century and it has the same secondary motif and main border as the *omurga göl* carpet illustrated in plate 5. The secondary border stripe of small reciprocal triangles is also specific to the Saryk and Ersari.

A SARYK ENSI

It is not surprising that until the 1960s, there was disagreement about whether weavings such as that shown in plate 7 were made as decorative tent door curtains, as had been reported by travelers, or as prayer rugs. The adherents of the door theory found their view confirmed by a long-forgotten newspaper picture, published in 1885 and rediscovered by Neil Moran in 1985, that showed a Saryk ensi on a tent door.[28]

The Wiedersperg ensi, like the Salor trapping (see pl. 4), was published by Ulrich Schürmann[29] and is an early and esteemed example. Among specific features of Saryk ensis are the asymmetrically arranged field ornaments and field border, both with birds' heads, the prominent line of rectangles forming a border immediately below the field, and the well-drawn floral upper and lower elements. While most ensis made by the Tekke (see pls. 17 and 18), and one type made by the Arabachi (see pl. 53), have a single mihrab at the top (one reason that they were thought to be prayer rugs), Saryk ensis usually have between three mihrabs (the older examples) and seven. Other ensis, including those of the Salor and Yomut, have no mihrab. An

PLATE 7. Saryk door rug *(ensi)*

PLATE 8 (ABOVE). Saryk bag *(torba)*

PLATE 9 (RIGHT). Saryk(?) tent band *(ak yüp)* (fragment)

unusual feature is the fading from the intense red field color characteristic of other ensis of this generation. The fact that fading is rare is
supporting evidence that the ensis were generally made for weddings
and then put away rather than used and so exposed to the strong sun-
light of the region.

OTHER SARYK WEAVINGS

Saryk torbas are rare and very similar in design (although different
in structure and colors) to six-gul torbas made by the Tekke, the most
significant difference in drawing being in the interior of the *gul*s, a
diamond with *kochak*s (Turkish for "ram's horns") at the four points.
In common with a large proportion of Tekke torbas, the Saryk torba
has the kochanak border. The torba illustrated in plate 8 entered the
collection in 1978.[30]

Surviving Saryk tent bands are also rare. The Wiedersperg Collection contains a length of what must have been an outstanding example (see pl. 9), exceptionally fine in weave and in the silk-like quality
of its wool. However, it must be remembered that since most tent
bands are similar in structure, unless there are tribe-specific designs,
tribal attributions depend on color shades and remain uncertain.

The Tekke

Abul Ghazi first mentions the Tekke as joint descendents with the
Saryk from a Salor ancestor Toy Tutmaz and, together with the
Saryk and the Yomut, as comprising the Outer Salor in the late six-
teenth century.[31] The Tekke are mentioned as part of the Turkmen

of the Balkhan Mountains in the early seventeenth century and, with the Ali-eli, Imreli, and Yomut at Neza and Durun, as being defeated by Nadir-shah in the first half of the eighteenth century. In 1740 the Tekke were reported as fighting side by side with the Yomut and Uzbek.[32] The Tekke are said to have left the Balkhans during the eighteenth century and occupied the Akhal region under their leader Keymir Ker.[33] In the nineteenth century, a part of the tribe migrated to Tejen and were reported as fighting with the help of the Salor to occupy Merv in 1843. They occupied Sarakhs in 1855 and Merv in 1857, evicting the Saryk entirely in 1859.[34]

There are earlier reports on what may have been the same tribe in Anatolia. Between 1260 and 1340 the Ghazi leaders who organized the Turkmen tribes in western Anatolia founded independent principalities or emirates that became united under Osman Ghazi (after whom the Ottoman Turks are named) after he had defeated the Byzantine army in Nicaea (Iznik) in 1302.[35] Tekke was the name of one of these independent regions in southwest Anatolia,[36] but it is not clear whether the region took on a tribal name or vice versa. At the end of the fifteenth century, the so-called Tekkeli (that is, belonging to the Tekke tribe) supported the Safavids in Central Anatolia and were one of the eight Turkmen tribes that joined Shah Ismail at Erzincan in Eastern Anatolia in 1499. Whether the Central Asian and Anatolian histories speak of the same Tekke tribe and how this relates to the close similarity and even identity of designs and ornaments of some fifteenth-century Anatolian and eighteenth- and nineteenth-century Central Asian Turkmen rugs is still an open question.

TEKKE MAIN CARPETS

Before World War II, Tekke main carpets were sold under the name "Bokhara" and were often called "gentlemen's carpets." The Tekke were the most prolific of all Turkmen weavers and yet—although many tens of thousands of Tekke carpets have been woven in different sizes, qualities, and different shades of red, for the tent or house or for the market, over at least the past four centuries—the field decoration of all has consisted of between four and seven vertical rows of Tekke göls offset against rows of one of three different secondary güls.

The field decoration is based on a composition of compartments formed by vertical and horizontal lines that pass through the centers of the göls (see fig. 1B). A second compartment structure, which overlaps the first, is formed through the secondary güls by bands that, rather than being explicitly drawn, are created in the mind by extrapolation from the cross shapes of either of the two minor ornaments, as may be seen in the *chemche güls* in the carpets illustrated in plates 10, 11, and 12 or the *kurbaghe* gul in plate 13.

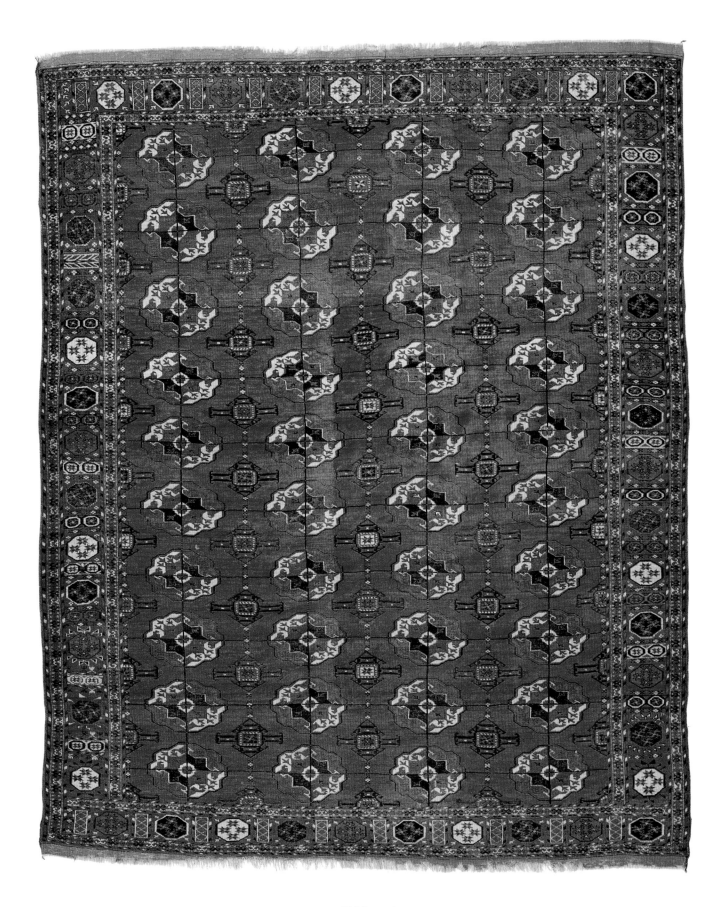

PLATE 10. Tekke main carpet

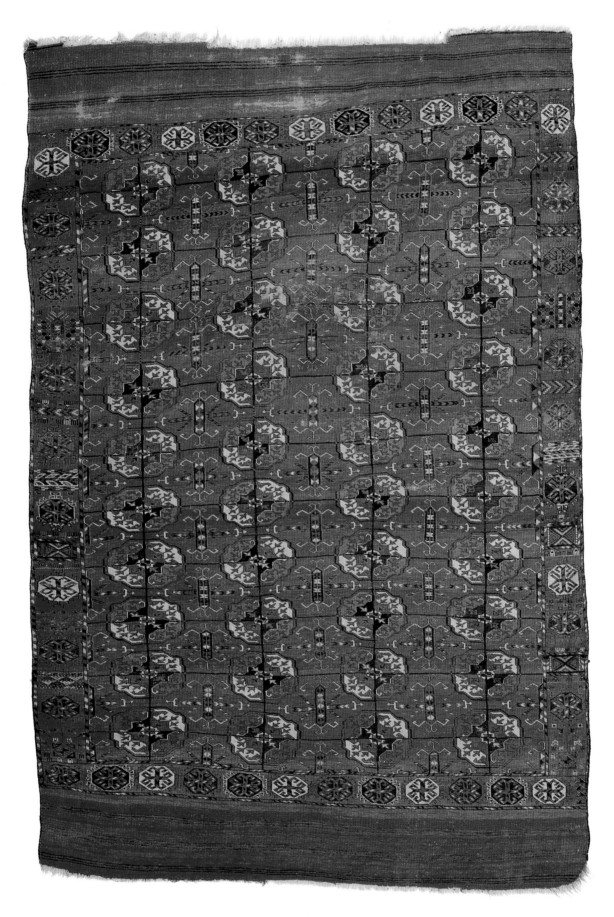

PLATE II. Tekke main carpet

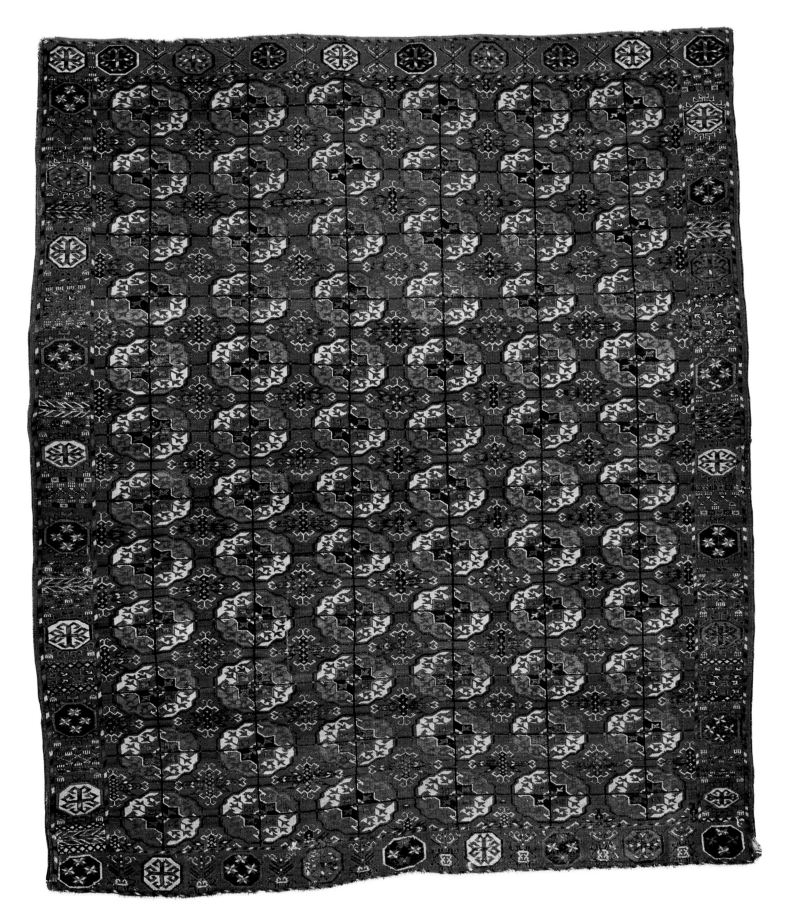

PLATE 12. Tekke main carpet

PLATE 13. Tekke main carpet

This double-compartment structure, with roundels and cruciform ornaments in the interstices, is ubiquitous and has been used in endless repeat surface designs for almost four thousand years. The earliest known examples are on ceiling drawings in Theban tombs in Egypt dating from the early and mid-second millennium B.C. It is seen in manifold variations in Sasanian, T'ang, and Byzantine textiles of the first millennium A.D., in groups of classical late-medieval Eastern Mediterranean and Anatolian carpets, in nineteenth-century carpets from Persian Kurdistan, in *suzani*s (embroideries) from east Uzbekistan (Tashkent), and even in twentieth-century neckties and wallpaper.

In the Near and Middle East the number forty often stands for "many," and because most old Tekke carpets, such as those shown in plates 10 and 11, have forty well-spaced *göl*s (four across and ten down), the classical Tekke carpet has sometimes been taken to represent this number. Among other features regarded as early are a minor border with reciprocal kochak motifs (see pl. 10) or a single guard stripe and no minor borders (as may be seen in pl. 10), and pile rather than flatwoven alems (also pl. 11).

The number of rows of *göl*s in a Tekke carpet does not provide evidence of its age, but may indicate a particular group. The carpets shown in plates 11 and 12 have very different ground colors, but both have six rows of twelve *göl*s, and a close relationship between the carpets is demonstrated by the similarity in drawing of the *chemche* guls, the alternation of the internal decoration of the octagon in the main border, the absence of minor borders, and in the short borders, the unusual intermediate motifs between octagons.

An interesting relationship exists among different Tekke knotted-pile weavings. Early main carpets, ensis, and torbas tend to be made of wool yarn of four dyed colors, red, orange, blue, and green, together with natural, undyed ivory and brown; old Tekke chuvals, kaps, and *kapunuk*s (door surrounds) have a less restricted palette.

SMALL TEKKE RUGS

Early examples of small Turkmen rugs are rare, and because their function in the tradition is unclear, the literature has for the most part ignored their existence. The fragment shown in plate 14 was woven with a chuval gul and with border ornaments that are miniature versions of those of Tekke main carpets. Plate 15 illustrates a structurally intact but heavily worn small rug that is as finely woven as most chuvals but is of a type that may, as has been recently suggested, have played a role in weddings. Plate 16 shows what seems to be a fragment of a small rug, although it has the *göl*s of a main carpet and a pile alem like that of the main carpet shown in plate 11.

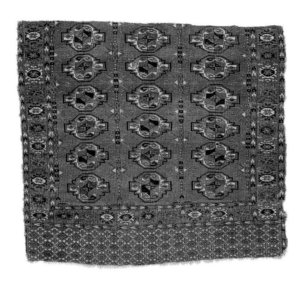

PLATE 14. Tekke rug (fragment)

PLATE 15. Tekke rug

PLATE 16. Tekke rug (fragment)

TEKKE ENSIS

In the West, up to about 1950, the Tekke ensi was frequently sold as a "Princess Bokhara" and, because it has a *mihrab* shape at the top, like prayer rugs from other regions, it was assumed to be a prayer rug. From growing evidence in the carpet and travel literature, we now know that the ensi was used as a tent door hanging. This is confirmed by the fact that the ensis of the Salor and the Yomut tribes are woven without a mihrab, and those of the Saryk and others have a row of mihrabs at the top, which in some cases is clearly related to the kejebe design that is identified with the Turkmen wedding rather than with Islamic prayer.

This evidence does not, however, answer all the questions. The photographs and drawings of Turkmen yurts that were published in the early literature show the doors of yurts closed with felt. Why, if ensis were regularly exposed to the bright Central Asian sun, did so few show faded colors? Did the seminomadic and the settled Turkmen use ensis in houses? And why, after all, did some ensis look so much like prayer rugs?

It is likely that the ensi was part of the paraphernalia that accompanied the bride on her traditional wedding caravan. It was placed over the door of the new tent and then, with the asmalyks and other trappings, put away after the wedding. This, of course, leaves room for those who like to speculate that the Tekke and Arabachi ensis (see pl. 54), with their single mihrab, may have been used later, on the floor as prayer rugs or on the wall as precious keepsakes or icons.

Although there is much that we do not know for certain about the use of ensis, we have learned a good deal about the designs and ornaments of Tekke examples, and it is possible to distinguish three types. The survival of quite large numbers of very similar Tekke ensis, compared with the very small number of earlier and more variable examples, suggests that, possibly from as early as 1870, Tekke ensis, like the Saryk example shown in plate 7, were woven in the Merv Oasis for the market rather than for the weaver's own use.

A few Tekke ensis with the so-called animal-tree design have survived.[37] Although this group includes both very early ensis and late examples dyed with the synthetic azo dye Ponceau 2R, which came into use in Turkmenistan in the early 1880s, the design has remained stable into modern times. A third group of early Tekke ensis, also relatively small in number, is distinguished by designs that are both much more variable and more colorful. The ensis shown in plates 17 and 18 are of this type. Within the context of a stable Turkmen tradition, they are extraordinary, magnificent, and individualistic works of the imagination.

TEKKE CHUVALS

Most Tekke chuvals have one of three designs, and the Wiedersperg Collection includes representatives of two. As far as can be judged by the evidence of the surviving pieces, the Salor or Mary gul (see fig. 11) appears to have been used on chuvals by weavers from the same Turkmen tribes (that is, the Salor, Tekke, Saryk, and Ersari) that also used the *gushly* (or *gülli*) *göl* on their main carpets. The design of the gul (also referred to as the turreted gul) is related to that of the medallions on Turkish carpets of the large-pattern Holbein type (so named because they can be seen in the paintings of the German artist Hans Holbein [ca. 1465–1524] and his contemporaries). The name Salor gul comes from a period in which a generation of the carpets made by the Tekke of the Merv Oasis was attributed to the Salor, thus the designation Mary gul in some sources, after Mary, the largest city on the oasis.

PLATE 17. Tekke door rug *(ensi)*

PLATE 18. Tekke door rug *(ensi)*

PLATE 19. Tekke bag *(chuval)*

When we compare the early Tekke chuval in plate 19 with the Salor chuval shown in plate 2, we see that, except for the "flag" border (named, presumably by a British author, because of its resemblance to the British flag), which is specific to the Tekke, the designs are identical. Only a few Tekke chuvals of the type have survived, and we do not know whether this design was copied from the Salor or whether both came from a common source. In the Tekke version, the design changed over time to show two whole rows of the Salor guls. Other chuvals, probably dating from the first half of the nineteenth century or before, tend to show an alem with the ring-tree design that is specific to Tekke chuvals. Chuvals with Salor guls were made well into the twentieth century, and in late examples the interior elements of both major and minor guls show considerable variations, and the number of major *göl*s may rise to nine.

Weavers from all Turkmen tribes have produced chuvals with one or more variations of the chuval gul. Among Tekke chuvals, the gul layout is not fixed, most having between twenty (four by five) and thirty (five by seven) small guls. A few, mainly early pieces, have only twelve (three by four) somewhat larger guls. In plate 20 the field of four by four guls is framed by a geometric compartment border, and

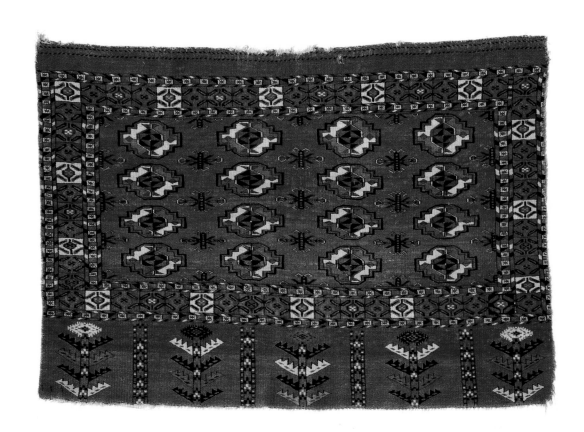

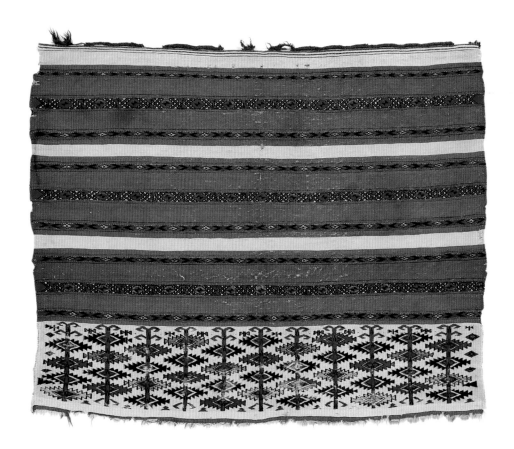

PLATE 20 (ABOVE). Tekke bag *(chuval)*

PLATE 21 (BELOW). Tekke bag *(ak chuval)*

the alem has a version of the tree design that is shared with some Yomut chuvals. A third design used widely on Tekke knotted-pile chuvals is the *ayna* gul (see fig. 14).[38]

The *ak chuval* (*ak* is Turkmen for "white") is made with stripes of knotted pile alternating with wider red flatwoven stripes and a pile alem in white cotton or, more rarely, in silk. Felkerzam and Moshkova have illustrated ak chuvals from Merv, and the same technique has been reported by Dudin as being used for chuvals, kaps, and *khurjin*s (double or donkey bags) in both Merv and Akhal.[39] The Yomut and Göklen of northern Iran use storage packs, flatwoven and with stripes of brocading, that were made in pairs for loading on animals and stacked in tiers in the tent, where the brocading prevented them from slipping.[40] Ak chuvals do not have borders, but braided ropes are usually fixed at the sides.

Like almost all ak chuvals, that shown in plate 21 has six broad, undecorated bands, six medium bands with a diamond pattern, and six narrow bands, of which three are densely decorated with lattice or hexagon designs and three are more sparsely decorated. The alem is decorated with trees drawn through *ashik*s offset horizontally and terminating in, alternately, one or two kochaks. An unusual feature is that, as in Turkmen tent bands, offset knotting is used with asymmetrically knotted pile to draw the steep diagonal lines in the pile bands.

The few published pieces with the horizontal format, structure, and chevron design of plate 22[41] have been thought to be bags, but because this example lacks its lower end we cannot be certain. A similar chevron design is also known on brocaded rugs that have been attributed to a number of tribes.

FIG. 14. Detail of a Tekke chuval showing the *ayna* gul

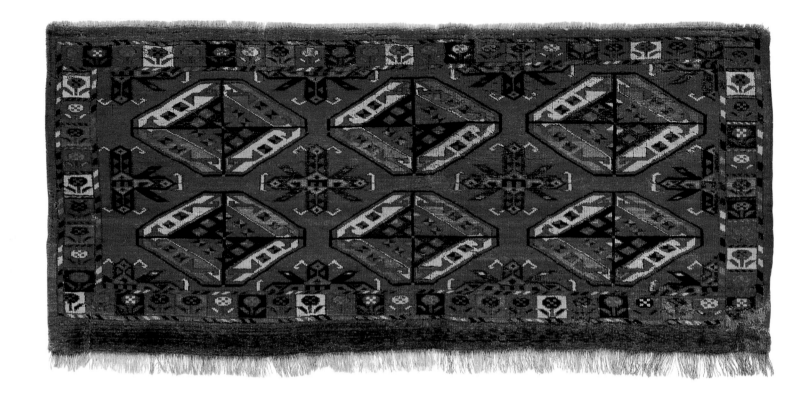

PLATE 23. Tekke bag *(torba)*

TEKKE TORBAS

The guls that decorate Tekke torbas differ from the chuval gul in shape and in their complex zoomorphic interior drawing. Tekke torbas can have six (two by three), twelve (three by four) or, rarely, nine (three by three) guls. However, we have no clear evidence of the origin of the guls on this torba except that it is also found on a number of main carpets that may be associated with the Yomut. Azadi has attributed the gul to the Karadashli tribe without, however, stating his evidence.[42] The rare and beautiful torba design shown in plate 23 is a variant example of a group of mainly six-gul torbas; the floral compartment border is fairly common on Tekke examples.

TEKKE KAPUNUKS

The "curled-leaf" ornament on a white ground is a symbol of growth and fertility and on Turkmen rugs it is used on borders of ensis, asmalyks, and main carpets[43] and as a field ornament on trappings. Its strongest association is, however, with the kapunuk (or *gapylyk*) and it is found on almost all the door surrounds of every Turkmen tribe, with the exception of the Yomut.[44]

The Wiedersperg Collection includes two Tekke kapunuks, both probably from the first half of the nineteenth century. They are similar in design and ornament, but have some slight though visually important differences. The example shown in plate 24 has arms with pointed ends and somewhat brighter reds; that in plate 25 has

PLATE 24 (ABOVE). Tekke door surround *(kapunuk)*

PLATE 25 (BELOW). Tekke door surround *(kapunuk)*

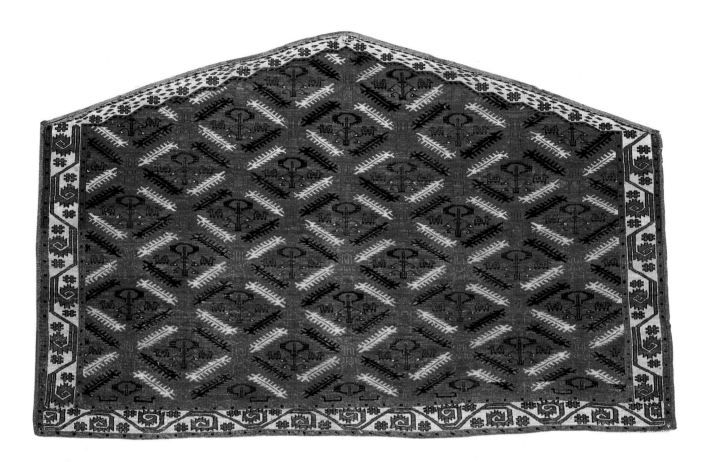

PLATE 26. Tekke wedding
trapping *(asmalyk)*

squared ends and a more restrained palette. Along the top of both
door surrounds, outlines form five reciprocal half-hexagons, but
their relationship to the similar design in the arms is clearer in plate
25. The curled leaves in the kapunuk in plate 25 are less broad, and
the subsidiary ornaments, two ashiks and several small triangular
comb amulets, are smaller and more spaciously arranged than those
in plate 24.

A TEKKE ASMALYK

Somewhat larger than most other Tekke asmalyks, with five lattice
compartments in the width, the impressive features of the "animal-
tree" asmalyk illustrated in plate 26 are its classical format and pro-
portions and the perfection of its drawing.[45] Highly unusual and extremely rare for any tribal weaving is the achievement by the weaver
of almost perfect symmetry in the animal-tree ornaments at the sides
of the piece and within the corners of both the field and the border.

A COMPOSITE RUG

Plate 27 shows a rug made up of five sections of a tent band that have
been sewn together. At a total length of thirty-five feet, the tent band

PLATE 27. Rug made from five pieces of Tekke tent band lengths

must have been almost complete. In such bands (*ak yüp*)[46] the white ground is of warp-faced plain weave and the colored designs in knotted pile. The ornamental vocabulary of tent bands differs radically from that of other objects woven with knotted pile, and the structure—consisting of symmetrical knots tied over alternate warps; i.e., tied on the raised warps of an open shed— is similar for examples of all tribes, making tribal attributions difficult and often uncertain. This finely woven piece, tentatively attributed to the Tekke, exhibits an extraordinary versatility, with sixteen different designs varying from the restrained to the explosive and including ornaments with intriguing interior motifs.

The Eagle *Gül* Groups

Some Turkmen carpets that cannot be attributed to a specific tribal group are named for elements of the design. The eagle gul carpets are among them. The name eagle gul comes from Bogulyubov, to whom the lower part of the ornament resembled the spread wings of an eagle (see figs. 4A–B),[47] and it was adopted by the Rautenstengels, whose painstaking analysis of the design and structure of the accessible examples was published in 1990.[48] The eagle gul itself, like some other Yomut carpet ornaments, is not readily seen as a *göl* in the sense in which we have used the term. Is it a foreign intruder into a Turkmen carpet? It may be, but even if it is a derivation from a Persian palmette, Bogolyubov would surely have agreed that the Turkmen have added to its magnificence.

The Rautenstengels classified a total of twenty main carpets into three groups, seven carpets in group I, eleven in group II, and three in group III. The analysis also turned up one main carpet with the eagle gul group II design that was woven with the symmetrical knot. Later work by the Rautenstengels and others has identified chuvals, torbas, asmalyks, trappings, and tent bands of the three groups. The tribal affiliation of the eagle gul weavings has proved difficult to ascertain. Bogolyubov's original attribution of a carpet in the Rautenstengels' group II to the Yomut has been taken up by other authors and has much to commend it. Azadi's attribution of group I to the Göklen is not universally accepted, although there is some evidence to support it. No affiliation for group III has been proposed.

EAGLE GUL MAIN CARPETS

The differences between carpets of groups I and II are pronounced, beginning with the eagle guls, which differ in shape and interior drawing. In group I rows of *dyrnak göls* separate the first and last rows of four eagle guls from the end borders; in group II rows of

PLATE 28. Eagle *gul* main carpet, group II

PLATE 29. Eagle *gul* main carpet, group III

three eagle guls begin and end the field design. There are also differences between the borders of group I and II carpets and sometimes quite striking differences in colors.[49]

The differences in construction are no less significant. The asymmetrical knot in carpets of group I opens to the left and, in group II, to the right, and the average knot density is higher for group I. In the main carpets of this group we also see a more complex weft sequence and yarn composition, with three wool yarns to every yarn of silk. The wefts in group II main carpets are of wool and cotton. The pile yarn in group II carpets, as in most Turkmen carpets, is predominantly of Z2 wool, while in group I carpets it is regularly of Z3 or Z4.

The group II carpet illustrated in plate 28 is one of two previously unknown examples that bring the known number surviving up to thirteen. By coincidence, both the newly discovered carpets have the strong, bright colors of an old carpet that has been stored away from light for most of its life. If we look at this carpet as a *dyrnak göl* Yomut carpet with regular alternate rows of major *göl*s (with anchorlike or flower motifs in the corners) and minor *gül*s (simpler and a little smaller), we see that the eagle guls comprise every second horizontal row of major *göl*s.

The three carpets of the Rautenstengels' small group III, one of which is illustrated in plate 29,[50] can best be understood in relation to carpets of the two other groups, its features being somewhat less uniform. The eagle gul shape and field layout here are similar to those of group I carpets, but the number of guls per row varies (three in this example). The borders are more similar to, although not identical with, group I carpets. The compostion of the weft varies: all wool in the carpet illustrated, but wool, silk, and cotton in the other two. In all group III carpets the knot is open on the left (as it is in group I) and in knot density they are closer to group II. As it is in group I, the pile yarn in group III carpets is usually Z3. In some respects group III would seem to be a variable hybrid form, although the carpets tend to be similar to those of group I in some important details. It is likely that they were woven later or at a place somewhat distant from the source of the more uniform group I carpets.

AN EAGLE GUL CHUVAL

Plate 30 illustrates a group II eagle gul chuval of elaborate design, which includes a full-shaped gul with cleft sides and *giyak* (barber's pole) guard stripes at one side of the so-called "running dog" minor border.[51] The most striking ornament and one that is specific to a group of eagle gul chuvals is the row of five elaborately drawn vases holding what might be five-blossomed flowers in the broad alem.

The Yomut

PLATE 30. Eagle *gul* bag
(chuval), group II

Although the Yomut suffered greatly at the hands of the Persians during the reign of Nadir-shah,[52] and some resettled far to the north around Khiva, the people of this loose tribal grouping were certainly the most Persianized of the Turkmen tribes, and elements of this cultural affinity can be seen even in nineteenth-century carpets, particularly those described as main carpets. Areas such as Sarakhs, Merv, and the narrow strip of arable land north of the Kopet-Dagh were periodically under Persian suzereignty, but the Yomut settlements in the basins of the Atrek and Gorgan Rivers, which border the southeastern corner of the Caspian Sea, were long controlled by the Persian shah. Here many Yomuts have lived for centuries, and the environs of one city, Astrabad, were populated to some extent by sedentary Yomuts and related tribes.

Indeed, Yomut habitation has long extended along the southeastern shores of the Caspian in the direction of modern Krasnovodsk (now known as Türkmenbashy). These people have taken a major part in the trans-Caspian maritime trade, and models of Turkmen boats used in this trade are to be found in the History Museum in Ashkhabad. Turkmen were also engaged in commercial fishing in the Caspian, and at one point the Jafarbai Yomut subtribe occupied the island of Cheleken.[53] In general one might describe these Yomut as among the most settled of Turkmen. The Atabai and Jafarbai have been the largest tribal divisions during the last century, but there are many other distinct subtribes. Not surprisingly, these Persianized Yomuts seem to have a long tradition of carpet weaving. Recent Yomut main carpets from northeastern Iran—even those with the common *kepse* and *dyrnak guls*—may be either symmetrically or asymmetrically knotted; older Yomut main carpets are, for the most part, symmetrically knotted.

The Polish Jesuit missionary Father Krusinski, who spent twenty-five years in Persia at the beginning of the seventeenth century, wrote specifically about workshops that had been established by Shah Abbas throughout the empire for the production of luxury goods, including carpets, for the court.[54] He mentioned such major cities as Kashan and Mashad and the Shirvan and Karabagh regions. The exact location of the Karabagh workshops has not been identified —suggestions range from Shusha to Gendje—but the hundreds of surviving large rugs, including the dragon rugs and related afshan and harshang rugs of the seventeenth and eighteenth centuries, are thought to have been woven there. The attention of few carpet scholars, however, has been focused upon Krusinski's reference to Astrabad as the location of another court workshop. This city lies in a region inhabited by large numbers of Yomuts as well as Persians. The exact tribal composition of the Turkmen residing in and around Astrabad at the time is discussed by Barthold.[55] Not only were there Yomut and Göklen elements in that area, but also another Turkmen group known as the Sayin-Khani. That they were influential in the city is suggested by the fact that, on several occasions, Turkmen were appointed by the shah to be local governors. In the opinion of the authors, the possibility of a workshop in Astrabad should be given thoughtful consideration in light of Krusinski's subsequent remark that "each place was to weave in its own manner."[56]

One could assume that no rugs from any such workshop have survived, and it is difficult to imagine just what a seventeenth-century workshop rug from Astrabad would look like. We should remind ourselves, however, that it need not necessarily have been something for use in the Safavid court—as surely such types as the dragon rugs were not intended for use in Isfahan—but much material from the workshops was intended to provide income for the shah. Consequently we need not assume that any rugs from the Astrabad workshop, which we have adequate reason, based on Krusinski's account, to believe existed, would necessarily be in particularly large sizes destined for use in, for example, the Chehel Sutun, the shah's large reception pavilion in Isfahan. Nor would the designs be any more faithful to Persian originals than are the designs of rugs from the Karabagh or

Shirvan workshops. In Caucasian rugs we see elaborate Persian floral palmettes reduced to relatively crude, scarcely recognizable forms.[57] Might there have been any equivalent forms from Yomut or other Turkmen rugs that could have been woven in the Astrabad workshop or in the environs of Astrabad?

There are a few rugs that might have come from those workshops, specifically four pieces on which the decorative elements appear to be intermediate between Persian floral forms and guls found on more recent Yomut rugs. One major piece is in the Ballard Collection in the Metropolitan Museum of Art, another was first published by Schürmann, a third, from the Wher Collection, was published by Thompson, and the fourth, in the Hecksher Collection, is perhaps most archaic of all.[58] Jon Thompson has pointed out forms intermediate between Persian palmettes and the *kepse* gul to be found on Yomut rugs such as that shown in plate 33.[59] Forms ancestral to the "C" gul (pl. 31) may also be seen on the Ballard carpet. The eagle gul (see pls. 28 and 29) is probably the modern form that is most clearly related to the Persian palmette; similar forms may be seen on eighteenth-century Caucasian rugs that were also based on Persian originals.

We can reasonably theorize that rugs from the seventeenth- or eighteenth-century Astrabad workshop quite plausibly could have shown adaptations of extremely complex Persian floral forms. When we find descendants of these renditions on nineteenth-century Yomut main carpets, we can suggest that they may well have been strongly influenced by the output of the Astrabad workshop, just as such nineteenth-century Caucasian rugs as the sunburst, the kasim ushag, and palmette rugs such as the so-called Lenkoran, were obviously influenced by the dragon rugs and their relatives that many believe to be the output of the court looms in the Caucasus. But is it possible that actual rugs from the Astrabad workshop survive? On this we can only speculate. The Hecksher rug has been carbon dated to the seventeenth century,[60] and the Ballard rug in many respects seems substantially earlier than the generation of Yomut main carpets seen in the Wiedersperg Collection.

Eagle gul rugs, especially those of group II, have unusual structural features that might suggest an origin in the seventeenth century or even earlier and a connection with an urban workshop. (Silk wefts seem unlikely in the work of nomads, who would not be expected to grow their own silk.)[61] Under these circumstances—when the gul may well be based upon an urban decorative form—the use of the word *göl* (in reference to a tribal emblem) is clearly problematic.

YOMUT MAIN CARPETS

The eagle gul rugs in the Wiedersperg Collection (see pls. 28 and 29) have been considered separately. Among the other main carpets in the collection, the "C" gul example (shown in pl. 31) is particularly

PLATE 31. Yomut main carpet

PLATE 32. Yomut main carpet, reconstructed from fragments

noteworthy, because the figures between the *guls* are especially prominent. Sienknecht[62] has divided these carpets into groups relating to the presence or absence of other types of guls and the orientation of the guls. This example shows a diagonal orientation resulting from differences in color within the guls. The border is a simple curled-leaf variant in which the leaf forms do not connect with the scrolling vines. To the extent that gul forms on Yomut rugs have any subtribal significance, it is likely that these rugs were woven by the same groups that produced many of the *kepse* rugs, as there are examples containing both gul types.

The collector rescued the rug illustrated in plate 32 from a company that, several decades ago, made a business of cutting up old rugs to make purses. Much of this example had been cut into pieces and required careful restoration. Several gaps were left from pieces that could not be recovered. The design includes a gul that shares some features with the typical "C" gul and the *kepse* gul (see pl. 33), and Sienknecht describes it as a "C" gul variant.[63] Here the more descriptive term serrated rosette gul is used. Several rugs have both a typical "C" gul and a *kepse*; some carpets may have even a third gul. When there are two or three different types of guls on a given carpet, one could theorize that a number of subtribes had merged, and thus the weavers used more than one gul or—probably more realistically—the elements were simply used for their decorative functions.

The main carpet shown in plate 33 has the *kepse* gul, but in a variant in which the guls are in an unusual arrangement. The guls of this type of rug are almost always arranged to form diagonal bands, but here the six guls with substantial areas of white—in two different color arrangements—interrupt the diagonals and create a different effect. The main border is a variant of the curled leaf, and the long skirts at both ends show a most unusual design.

The *dyrnak göl* as seen in plate 34 may have no tribal significance, particularly when it appears among the Chodor and Ersari, and it may appear as a minor ornament on other types of rugs as well. Similar lozenge-shaped structures with latchhooks even appear on rugs from Turkey and on various types of Persian tribal rugs. This does not preclude the possibility that these ornaments have taken on a particular significance to the groups using them. The alems of this main carpet show a motif (the *erre* gul) that also appears as a minor gul on asmalyks and bags. Although various names have been attached to the design of the main border, it is likely derived from a vine border on Persian floral rugs. This *dyrnak* rug shows two distinctly different types of lozenge-shaped gul; in others the same *dyrnak* is varied by the distribution of colors. Some *dyrnak* rugs, like that on plate 34, show two distinctly different ornaments, a *göl* with anchorlike details, and a simpler and sometimes smaller minor *gül*.

*Göl*s with small animal figures in each quadrant are often

PLATE 33. Yomut main carpet

PLATE 34. Yomut main carpet

PLATE 35. Yomut main carpet

described by the term *tauk nuska* or variants ranging as far afield as *tavuk muska,* each with different possible meanings. The animal may have a clearly differentiated head and tail or there may be heads on both ends. The *göl* appears on Yomut, Chodor, Ersari, Kizil Ayak, and Arabachi Turkmen rugs and on others that are probably not woven by Turkmen. The figures may all be oriented in the same direction, or half the figures may be oriented in one direction and half in the other. On Turkmen rugs, these animal forms are often described as bird figures or as two-headed bird figures; the version that appears on the Karakalpak or Turkmen Uzbek pieces (see pls. 77 and 78) has a clearly delineated head, tail, and four legs.

The carpet in plate 35 has two different alem designs, both of which also appear on bag faces. The alems are missing from the carpet on plate 36, and the colors are less saturated, but the *göls* on the

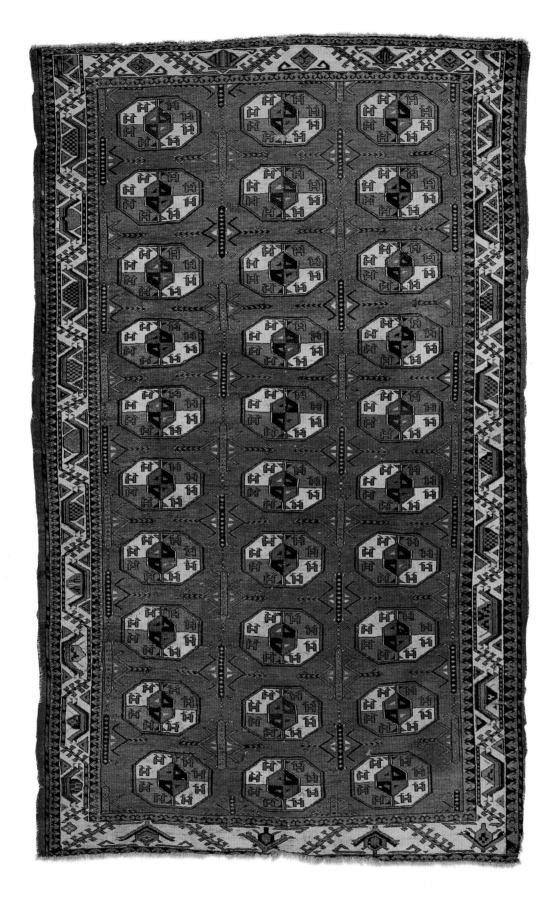

PLATE 36. Yomut main carpet

 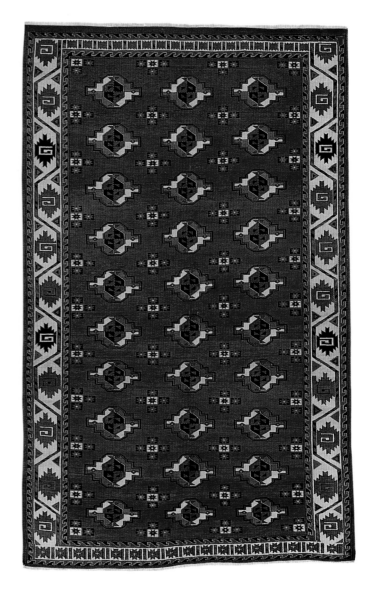

PLATE 37 (ABOVE LEFT).
Yomut main carpet

PLATE 38 (ABOVE RIGHT).
Yomut main carpet

two pieces are quite similar. The highlights around the minor gul in plate 35 create a much livelier effect than obtains in plate 36.

The main carpets shown in plates 37 and 38 both have guls ordinarily associated with bag faces, particularly chuvals. The minor gul to be seen in plate 38 is also a type that could appear on a bag face, although the small *dyrnak göl* on plate 37 would ordinarily be found only on a main carpet. The alems are lacking from the main carpet in plate 38, but bags with that combination of major and minor gul will often have an undecorated alem. The sparsely arranged figures in the alem in plate 37 could also appear on a bag face. The latchhook minor borders—identical on both rugs— are also commonly found on bag faces. The rug shown in plate 38 makes an austere impression; that in plate 37 seems much more lively.

A YOMUT ENSI

Yomut ensis show enormous variability. The ensi in plate 39, with two
alem panels at the bottom and no mihrab at the top, is a fairly common
variation. As in most other ensis, the field is quartered. A field covered
with diagonally arranged small decorative devices is common, as are
the rather stiff curled-leaf bands that form the central cross and en-
close the field. Some Yomut ensis, usually late, have an archlike figure
at the top of the central column. The strong colors and rather austere
drawing suggest a relatively early origin for this example.

YOMUT BAGS

There are three Yomut chuvals in the Wiedersperg Collection, including one flatweave. The chuval shown in plate 40 is the simplest

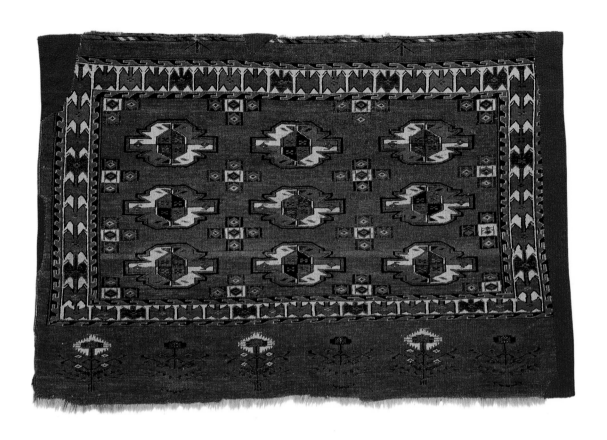

PLATE 40 (ABOVE). Yomut bag *(chuval)*

PLATE 41 (BELOW). Yomut bag *(chuval)*

PLATE 42. Yomut bag *(chuval)*

in concept but shows an interesting imbalance in the way some of the ornaments are arranged. The flowering plants in the alem show a certain asymmetry of color in their arrangement, and it is interesting to notice that the figures in the top and bottom main borders do not match in size or color. The guls are essentially identical except that light blue is used in the central figures of some and dark blue in others. The range of colors and especially the use of pale blue are effective features of the chuval shown in plate 41. This bag face gives the impression of being crowded with design, the apparent random placement of white highlights in the borders and alem producing a charming sense of asymmetry. We see here essentially the same minor gul that appears in plate 40, although here it is relatively more prominent.

The flatwoven chuval illustrated in plate 42 shows a finely rendered but rather static repetition of the same major and minor guls, with similarly repetitive border stripes. Most of the rigidity of the design is an effect of the patterning weave itself, supplementary-weft wrapping, which is a more restrictive structure than knotted pile.

The small bag shown in plate 43 is of a type usually described as a mafrash or kap and, with its symmetrical knotting and typical bag face guls, is correctly described as Yomut, although the minor guls resemble a miniature version of the Chodor *ertmen göl.*

PLATE 43. Yomut bag *(kap)*

The asmalyk is known—from early photos—to have been used on the flanks of the lead camel in a Turkmen bridal procession. The great majority of them are of Yomut origin. There are, however, rare but well-known Tekke types with bird and animal-tree figures and asmalyks made by the Ersari, Chodor, Saryk, and Arabachi (only one of the last named) have been identified. Of the three asmalyks in the Wiedersperg Collection, that illustrated in plate 44 is the most typical in design, and its symmetrical knotting places it in the same structural category as most of the Yomut main carpets. The design may be seen in a number of different ways, but if one chooses to see it comprising a number of ivory-field, lozenge-shaped compartments created by jagged, crossing diagonal lines, a distant relationship to the Tekke bird asmalyks becomes apparent. What is probably the second most common asmalyk design is illustrated in plate 45. Asymmetrically knotted examples are known, but this piece is woven with the symmetrical knot. The source of the treelike design is uncertain. The major border here resembles the outer border of the piece shown on plate 46, and the stripes in the field of the latter are composed of the same figures with one lateral arm pointing up rather than down. The third asmalyk (pl. 46) cannot properly be described as five-sided, as the upper arch arises from the top of a rectangle rather than from its sides. The knotting here is asymmetrical.

The *ok bash* is a small baglike object woven as one piece as shown in plate 47. The uses suggested in the Western literature are numerous.

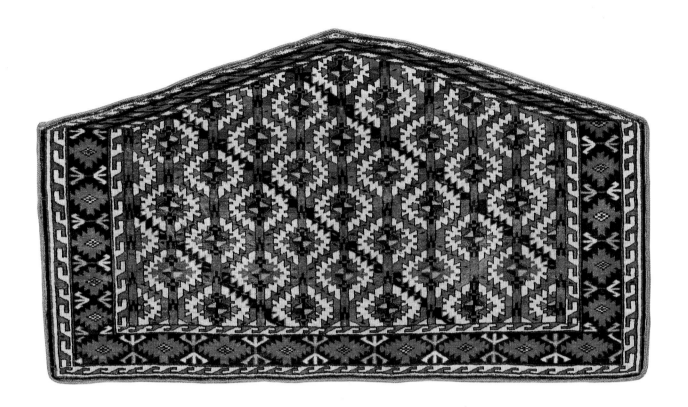

PLATE 44. Yomut wedding trapping *(asmalyk)*

PLATE 45. Yomut wedding trapping *(asmalyk)*

PLATE 46. Yomut wedding trapping
(asmalyk)

Because the word *ok* means "arrow" in Turkish, these pieces have been described as having descended from quivers, and in fact, a huntsman depicted on a Sasanian silver plate appears to be wearing a quiver with the chevron design of the type seen on the standard Turkman ok bash.[64] However, the Turkmen used ok bashs to cover the ends of tent poles in wedding caravans and during transport of the yurt. The weaving does not begin at the top edge of the bag, but at one of the sides, which are joined together to form the bag once the weaving has been removed from the loom. Consequently the triangular sections, which are sewn together to form the bottom of the bag, would actually have appeared along the one edge of the fabric when it was on the loom—in this case, the right edge, as determined by the direction of the pile. There is some variation in design among these pieces, but the ok bash shown on plate 48 is similar.

The Chodor

The first carpet published as a Chodor (by Bogolyubov as plate 23 in his text), had *göls* usually described by the term *ertmen*.[65] About three decades later, in 1934 and 1935, Moshkova surveyed Chodor villages in the Urgench region, where she reported the weaving of floor rugs, chuvals, and torbas.[66] Otherwise there are few early first-hand accounts of Chodor rugs, although these people played a part in early

Turkmen history, and they may have been among the earliest to settle into an agricultural existence.

One may read more or less reliable accounts of Turkmen movements during the past several centuries, but the important concept to remember is that ordinarily these people were reacting to external forces over which they had little control. When Persia was strong, as it was during the second quarter of the eighteenth century under Nadir-shah, Turkmen were pushed back from the Persian borders. When Persia was relatively weak, Turkmen moved southward, either uninvited or invited to help defend Persian borders. During periods of Kazak expansion, Turkmen were pushed to the south or east. As irrigation along the Amu Darya expanded, probably continually from the eighteenth century, Turkmen were allowed to settle and they became increasingly sedentary. During times of revolt or disorder in the emirates, they were either sought as allies or driven away. As the Russians moved into Central Asia, Turkmen either accommodated themselves to the changes or moved to Afghanistan or Iran. When one reads of Turkmen migrations from one place to another, it is useful to keep in mind that their power vis-à-vis the emirates, Persia, and eventually Russia was limited.

The Chodors had allegedly lived in the Mangishlak area before migrating, under pressure from Kazak expansion, to the south and east in the eighteenth century. A tribe known as the Javuldar (with variant spellings) was mentioned by early sources, and there has been speculation that, because of the similarity in name, this is a reference to the Chodor. Moshkova mentions their propensity for intermarriage with people of other tribes.[67] Many were settled in the Khiva emirate during the eighteenth and nineteenth centuries. Now large numbers live in the northern part of Turkmenistan, in the area around Urgench, Tashauz, and Khiva, and there are numbers south of Porsu along the Amu Darya, where they are bordered by Arabachi elements to the south.

CHODOR MAIN CARPETS

Chodor rugs are often recognizable at a glance by their colors, most prominently a deep mauve or purple color, usually for the field, and often set against a salmon red that in some rugs is quite pale. In other rugs red is the predominant color, and the purple becomes subsidiary. There is a relatively large amount of white, particularly for outlining, and both a light and dark blue are often found. Yellow is less prominent, but green is unusually common on a number of Chodors. The apricot color well known from the weavings of the Ersari, Tekke, Salor, and Saryk is almost unknown.

Structurally Chodor knotted-pile weavings all follow the same general specifications. They are asymmetrically knotted, open to the right, and the knot density ranges from relatively coarse (between 70 and 77 knots per square inch) as in the carpet shown in plate 50, to medium fine (between 153 and 162 knots per square inch) as in the chuval in plate 52, and nearly 200 per square inch in some chuvals. Moshkova indicates that some of these rugs are symmetrically knotted, but such pieces have not been seen by the authors. Moshkova also describes Chodor warps as made up of a goat-hair single plied with a single of camel hair or wool; wefts were usually of camel hair. The authors have been unable to confirm warp yarns of this description used in Chodor weaving, although occasionally yarns made up of two different materials are noted. The wefts are usually wool and cotton, often with one yarn of each per shot. Parts of a rug might have wefts entirely of wool, while, in rare cases, others might be entirely of cotton. Edges are often finished with a checkerboard selvage of brownish purple and salmon red; the plain-weave bands at each end are shorter than those found on Tekke, Salor, and Saryk rugs. There may be stripes, variable in size and organization.

Designs of Chodor main carpets are somewhat more varied than one finds among the Tekke, Salor, or Saryk. Some, which frequently appear to be slightly earlier—and usually smaller than typical Turkmen main carpets—show the *tauk nuska göl* (as in plate 49), often in slightly more saturated colors than are used in other Chodor main carpets.

Somewhat more common are Chodors with the *ertmen göl*, usually

PLATE 49. Chodor main carpet

PLATE 50. Chodor main carpet

arranged diagonally within a lattice, varying in color from row to row, and with no minor guls. Less often there are common variations of the hooked, lozenge-shaped *dyrnak göl*, there are renditions of the ashik and—on late carpets—of the kejebe design. The main carpet illustrated in plate 50 is extremely unusual in that it shows a human figure in the lower right corner.

Chuvals and torbas often exhibit the *ertmen göl*—at times a halved *ertmen* on torbas—but there are some chuvals with typical chuval guls. Whether these Chodor products reflect a rural or nomadic lifestyle is open to question. Large Chodor carpets are sometimes larger than the typical Turkmen main carpet, often exceeding ten feet, and several giant examples in excess of twenty feet are known.

OTHER CHODOR WEAVINGS

There are several types of Chodor prayer rugs and ensis,[68] but a relatively small number of prayer rugs, such as that illustrated in plate 51,

PLATE 51. Chodor prayer rug *(namazlyk)*

PLATE 52. Chodor bag *(chuval)*

have been identified. Only recently have several Chodor asmalyks been found.[69] There are torbas from Afghanistan with Chodorlike designs, but they often show colors more typical of recent Ersari or Kizil Ayak work. Chuvals with *ertmen* figures are common, although the one depicted in plate 52 shows a stronger red than would be expected, along with a slightly browner field color. The figures in the alem are more suggestive of a Yomut origin.

Chodor rugs continued to be woven well into the periods in which synthetic dyes were used. There is some reason to believe that at least some of these are workshop products from the region around Khiva and Urgench. Some recently published ideas about Chodor movements suggest that their designs have been greatly influenced by the various peoples around whom they have lived.[70]

The Arabachi

The labeling of rugs as Arabachi weavings is relatively recent in the West, although the term appears in earlier Soviet-era literature. Some Arabachi have, in recent times, lived in the vicinity of Denau just north of Chardjou on the Amu Darya, although small groups are scattered elsewhere. A group of Chodor also live north of the Arabachi, which may explain why there are some design similarities between rugs labeled as Chodors and others attributed to the Arabachi. Unlike Chodor rugs, however, Arabachi work shows asymmetrical knots open to the left, although they also often have cotton in the wefts, usually with one cotton and one wool strand plied together as a shot, which crosses twice between the rows of knots. Moshkova visited the area inhabited by the Arabachi in 1929 and noted that her expedition found, in the Arabachi village of Astana Baba, a rug with a *tauk nuska göl*.[71] She added that the Arabachis of this area considered this motif their own and used it to decorate rugs they wove for the market. Moshkova was also clear, however, that the *göl* was used by other groups as well and specifically commented upon its use by the Kizil Ayak.

ARABACHI MAIN CARPETS

The Arabachi customarily used the *tauk nuska göl* for their main carpets, and Arabachi examples with this design began to be recognized in the West in the 1970s. That shown in plate 53 is such a rug. At about the same time it also became clear that there were ensis and bags that showed an asymmetrical knot open to the left, some use of cotton in the weft, and the characteristic color tonality that included a dark brown field color with a purplish tinge. Arabachi main carpets with synthetic reds have been identified, suggesting that production continued well into the twentieth century; a pink shade has been found on ensis and tent bands and may occur on some main carpets as well.

AN ARABACHI ENSI

Arabachi ensis are known with two distinct designs. Both have a similar top panel incorporating a single mihrab and both have a camel train decorating a single-panel alem. In ensis of the best known type[72] the field is covered with a hexagon lattice, and white diamond shapes at the centers of the hexagons are threaded on parallel vertical white lines and form a diagonal cross. The ensi shown in plate 54 is in the more traditional of the designs. This is similar to the Tekke ensis (see pls. 18 and 20) with a quartered field decorated with rows of "candelabra" motifs and with the same outer border.

Various types of bags were also identified, and O'Bannon[73] depicts chuvals of the two main designs as well as a kap. One of the chuval designs shows a gul of the *gülli-göl* type that is almost identical to the *göl* on Tekke main carpets, except that its outer contours are more rounded. The only known asmalyk made by the Arabachi is illustrated in Bogolyubov.[74]

Rugs such as those depicted in plates 53 and 54 are certainly products of the Arabachi, but there are still a few unanswered questions.

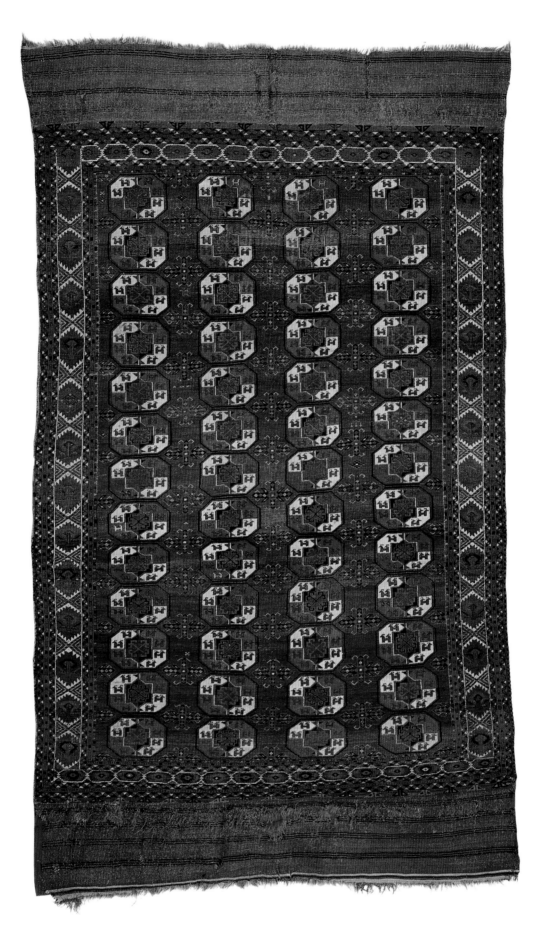

PLATE 53. Arabachi main carpet

PLATE 54. Arabachi door rug *(ensi)*

Relationships among other tribal groups can at least be formulated in outline, but the Arabachi present more of a challenge. They were referred to as an independent tribe by Abul Ghazi in the mid-seventeenth century,[75] although Moshkova described them as a sub-tribe of the Ersari, and others have thought of them as a subtribe of the Chodor whose rugs share with the Arabachi certain structural characteristics (frequent use of cotton in the wefts, for example) and some similarities in design and in palette.

The Ersari

There is some agreement about the relationships among the Tekke, Salor, and Saryk both in terms of their tribal origins and their weavings, which show certain similarities in design. The situation becomes murkier, however, when one considers the Ersari and their relationships with other Turkmen groups located along those stretches of the Amu Darya that separate Turkmenistan from Uzbekistan and in the border regions between Uzbekistan and Afghanistan. These peoples also inhabit parts of the Kashka Darya Valley around Karshi and areas west of the Amu Darya around Kerki, as well as some of the agricultural lands around Shibergan, Andkhui, and Maimana in northern Afghanistan. Moshkova provides descriptions of the subtribes and of groups of other tribal origin living among them along the middle reaches of the Amu Darya.[76]

Traveling in northern Afghanistan one still encounters groups that call themselves Chub Bash, Kizil Ayak, Charshango, Dali, Solimani, Saltiq, and numerous other designations, and there are towns in Uzbekistan and Afghanistan known by the names of some of these groups. There is some question about whether tribal names used in Afghanistan are simply designations of the regions from which those tribespeople migrated at some time in the past or whether they represent actual names of tribes. It is known that when the Russians established control over this part of Central Asia, many Turkmen groups migrated to northern Afghanistan for religious reasons, and around the time of the Russian revolution there were more tribal movements toward the south.

This complicates the issue of tribal identity, and it remains unclear just what the term Ersari means to those who use it. Does it refer to a specific tribal group, or is it a broader label for an assortment of subtribes? In some cases, the tribal history is clearer than in others. In 1641, Abul Ghazi wrote of his arrival in Meihane (in Balkhan among the Tekke) and his welcome there by the Kizil Ayak, which he described as a division of the Ersari, as did Bogolyubov 250 years later when the Kizil Ayak were at the Amu Darya. For other subtribes, such as the Chub Bash, Charshango, Dali, Solimani, and others, ethnographers have not convincingly answered this question, and it could be argued from several points of view.[77] One could say that many names of these Ersari-related people refer to subtribes or groups that migrated to Afghanistan, and the more common use of Ersari as an overall name for these peoples within what was the Soviet Union argues that at least there ethnic identity was not so complex. One could also contend that some Turkmen were living in northern Afghanistan well before Russian control was established north of the Amu Darya. It is also clear that in Afghanistan tribal names are used for various types of rugs that do not appear at all in the Soviet-era literature.

Despite a certain ambiguity in the labels, we have, however, decided to describe many of these rugs by the terms that have surfaced in the trade and seem to have become accepted by much of the scholarly community dealing with Turkmen rugs. In some respects this may be arbitrary and possibly inaccurate, but at least it allows communication among people who share the same vocabulary. Thus we will describe the Ersari group without any certainty that the rugs included in this section were all woven by peoples with any real connection to the Ersari. We will treat the objects with various other labels, such as Kizil Ayak and Chub Bash, as though they are the products of specific tribal groups related to the Ersari.

Whatever the actual kinship among these groups, their lives are similar, particularly as almost all live within the Amu Darya basin or near waterways that drain mountains to the west. No doubt as a result of the agricultural niche that this geography provides, these people have been relatively sedentary since the seventeenth century. There are remains of major Bronze Age settlements in this area, and ruins of Bactrian, Parthian, Sogdian, and Sasanian settlements are to be found in a region that probably had major Achaemenid towns as well. Clearly the region's agriculture has long been able to support a significant population, and when the Turkic people began to penetrate the region across the Syr Darya, it was inhabited by ancestors of the modern Tajiks, who make up a substantial part of the area's population and are the majority in nearby Tajikistan. Agriculture has probably been the major source of support for several millennia.

There are still tent-dwellers among the Ersari group, but most are sedentary, and the trappings of nomadic life may consequently form a relatively smaller part of the total woven output. Therefore we should not, perhaps, expect to find the same narrow range of sizes as we do, for example, among the main carpets of the Tekke, Salor, and Saryk. Carpets of the Ersari group are substantially more variable in size, with some pieces—apparently among the early surviving Turkmen rugs—far larger than the Tekke main carpet and clearly made for an urban environment.

As the areas where these were woven lay mostly within the Emirate of Bukhara, and some in the Emirates of Kokand and Khiva, it is

PLATE 55. Ersari main carpet

likely that the weavers enjoyed the patronage of town-dwellers for at least several centuries and to a greater extent than did the Tekke, Salor, and Saryk. Even now remnants of the early, traded rugs that we know as Beshir may be found occasionally in Bukhara, and with the arrival of the Trans-Caspian Railroad, a lively trade in these pieces developed.

ERSARI MAIN CARPETS

Quite distinct from the Beshir rugs made for town or city use are those woven for a nomadic or rural existence, which we are here describing as Ersari, although it is not certain that all the groups weaving such rugs could be considered as part of this tribal entity. The classic type here is the main carpet, which measures between about six feet ten inches and seven feet four inches by about eight feet two inches and nine feet six inches, and seems clearly analogous to main carpets woven by the Tekke, Salor, and Saryk. They are thick, relatively coarsely woven carpets, with large octagonal *gül*s and, usually, relatively simple minor guls. They have a major border, and some —often pieces that appear older—do not have guard stripes. Ends rarely show a knotted-pile skirt (such as that in plate 55), but more often have a kilim band of moderate width, with or without stripes. At times the stripes are multicolored.

As with Tekke main carpets, the same *göl*s have been used from the precommercial into the commercial period, and the designs have changed little. The differences are mostly in size, color, and regularity of the design elements. Later rugs are apt to be larger, more in keeping with the needs of Western rooms, and recent Ersari-type rugs with a repeating large-gul design—often described simply as Afghans—can be found in the traditional Western size, nine feet by twelve feet, or even larger. The pile is usually thick. The number of colors has tended to decline from the six or nine colors used in earlier rugs to sometimes only three or four in later rugs, although the guls will be drawn in a strikingly similar manner. White is less likely to appear later, or at least it will be in smaller amounts, and the subsidiary use of green, yellow, and light blue is less frequent. Some late rugs show stiffly drawn octagons spaced too closely together for there to be minor guls. The ends are likely to show no kilim band or only a very short one, and the edges—still usually reinforced with dark goat hair—are more likely to have a two- or three-rib selvage rather than the wider selvages of four or more ribs that are common on earlier rugs; that on the rug shown in plate 55 has a six-rib selvage.

The carpet illustrated in plate 55 appears to be the earliest of the complete Ersari rugs in the Wiedersperg Collection. The wool is lustrous and the colors particularly rich, with the *göl*s containing ivory arranged in diagonal lines. There is also a substantial amount of ivory in the border, which is probably an extremely degenerate Kufic

PLATE 56 (ABOVE LEFT).
Ersari main carpet

PLATE 57 (ABOVE RIGHT).
Ersari main carpet

form,[78] and an interesting variety of figures between guls. Note both the extra skirt stripe surviving at the bottom (there may originally have been one at the top as well) and the unusually wide, six-rib selvage of brown goat hair. In the rug shown in plate 56 the guls containing ivory are arranged in a 1-2-1-2-1 symmetry.

Among the surviving Ersari rugs of an obviously early vintage—presumably before 1880—one may still find much more variability than there is among the Tekke, Salor, and Saryk types. There are well over a dozen guls, and their significance in designating the work of a subtribe or some tribe other than the Ersaris is incompletely understood. The *göl* on the rug shown on plate 57, with three trefoils in each quadrant, is described as the *gülli göl* (as is the Salor main carpet *göl*), but Ersari rugs rarely have the animal figures that may be seen in the Salor version of this *göl* (see pl. 1).

The *göl* on the carpet in plate 58 is described as the *temirjin* or *omurga göl*, and it appears in a slightly different form on a small number of surviving early Saryk rugs rendered in the symmetrical knot. The absence of ivory in this example is not unknown on early Ersari rugs, and examples alleged to be from the Saltiq subtribe often show very little ivory.[79] The *gülli göl* in the fragment shown in plate 57 also shows virtually no ivory and unusually widely spaced guls. Here one sees a late form of the curled-leaf border. The fragment depicted in

PLATE 58. Ersari main carpet

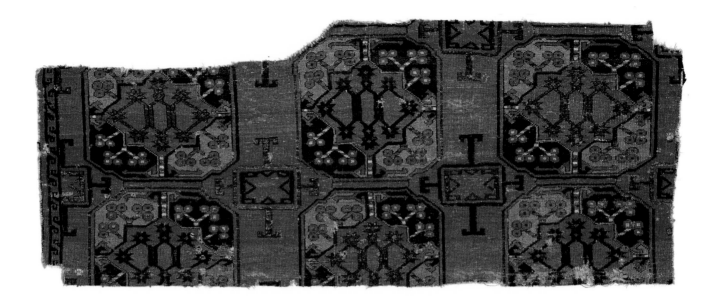

PLATE 59. Ersari main carpet (fragment)

plate 59 with a typical *gülli göl* shows an unusual and early minor *gül*. The rug itself is probably quite early and its border is of an unusual version of the curled-leaf type. This border occasionally appears on rare Tekke main carpets, where it, too, is assumed to be a particularly early feature.

Rugs from Afghanistan with a specific type of gul, colors, and textural characteristics are described as Chub Bash. In the West a specific color scheme has been identified with the Chub Bash. The main carpet show in plate 60 has a particularly dark purplish brown field, an unusually prominent use of green, and substantial ivory highlights, all regarded as characteristics of the type often called Chub Bash in the West. This may well be true, but its origins have not been confirmed. Notice that the minor gul of plate 60 is essentially the same figure that appears within the gul of plate 57. Despite the different minor guls, the rugs are similar enough to have been woven by the same small group.

ERSARI ENSIS, BAGS, AND TRAPPINGS

If one assumes that the earliest Ersari main carpets were made for use in a rural or nomadic environment, one would expect to find other weavings made for this life, including bags of various sorts, ensis, decorative trappings, and perhaps tent bands. A few Ersari asmalyks have been found, and there are several bags that have the same structure and colors as the gul-design main carpets, but their designs do not include the same guls that are to be found on main carpets. The weaving shown in plate 61, with a chuval format, has several types of border stripe and, in the alem, flowering plant forms that appear in flatwoven, red-field chuvals of the Yomut and in some chuvals with guls.

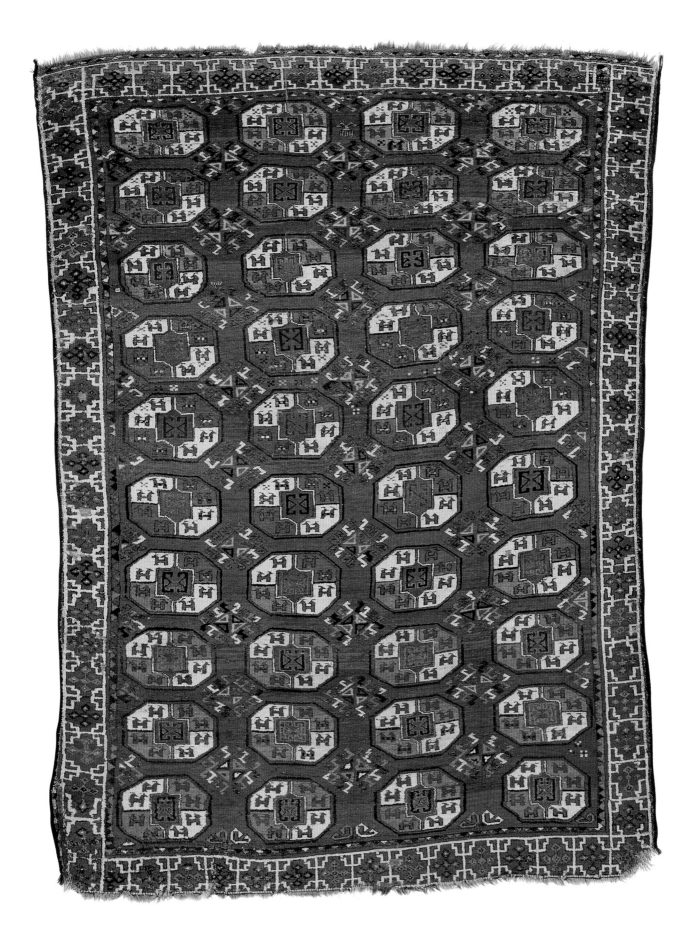

PLATE 60. Ersari or Chub Bash main carpet

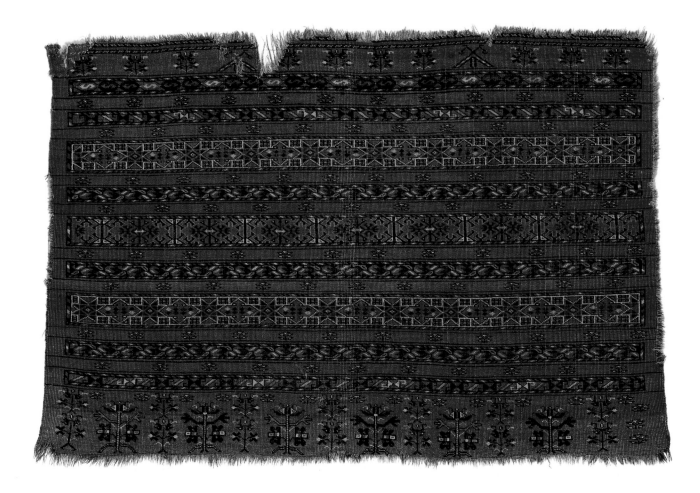

PLATE 61. Ersari bag *(chuval)*

Identification of the ensis provides a particular challenge, as several show some design elements—usually border stripes—that can be matched to border stripes on gul rugs. There are also ensis and main carpets that seem related by a similarity in texture and color tonalities. Some Ersari ensis show a small arch at the top of the central column and at times also on the column's lower half, as does that illustrated in plate 62. This example is unusual in having a design based on *ikat* in the horizontal panel of the central cross (see "Ersari bags with ikat-inspired designs" below). To date several Ersari *germech* have been found. These show designs related to the ensis and are believed to have been stretched across the bottom of the threshold. A number of rugs recently made in Afghanistan appear in ensi designs, but often these are particularly large (up to about five feet six inches by eight feet) and are clearly too big to be used as ensis.

ERSARI IKAT-INSPIRED DESIGNS

Ikat is a kind of silk or silk and cotton fabric in which the pattern is formed by binding and dyeing the warp before it is woven, producing a characteristic blurring at color boundaries. During the nineteenth century, ikats were popular throughout Central Asia for clothing for

PLATE 63. Ersari bag *(chuval)*

PLATE 64. Ersari bag *(chuval)*

both men and women, and numerous early photographs survive showing various local dignitaries dressed in flowing robes known as *chapan*s of this rich fabric. The designs are of a specific type that can be easily recognized when adapted to another weave.

During the nineteenth century, the Ersari and related groups made rugs that showed obvious elements of ikat design. There has been some controversy about whether to label these as Ersari or Beshir pieces, with some insisting that the ikat is not a tribal design and therefore the rugs should have the Beshir label. Most of the rugs, however, show the dark brown goat hair selvages common to Ersari rugs—but not to those pieces that we do label as Beshir—nor do they show the characteristic color variations of many Beshirs. Some other rugs show characteristics of both groups and cannot clearly be labeled as Ersari or Beshir with any degree of certainty.

The Wiedersperg Collection contains several objects with ikat-inspired designs. The most obvious is the chuval shown in plate 63, which remains close in color, detail, and effect to its original source (see fig. 15). Because the design has been translated into the medium of knotted pile, much of the fluidity associated with ikat has, however, been lost, and the design has become more regularized. In plate 64 one can see some color changes that would not be likely in an ikat, and the borders have designs unrelated to ikats. A relatively finely rendered ikat design is illustrated in plate 65, and there are surviving ikat fabrics showing many similar features, although the stylized floral forms within the eight compartments could not have been accomplished in the ikat technique.

Perhaps the most interesting use of ikat designs is found on the large fragments (pls. 66 and 67) that look as though they could be pieces of the same rug. Structural examination indicates they are not, and they were not obtained from the same source. They have a particularly early feel to them—quite apart from their having received heavy wear—and are not easy to assign to either the Beshir or to rural Ersari groups. These pieces show the same brown goat-hair selvage to be found on the gul rugs; most pieces of the Beshir group show the

FIG. 15. Ikats of this type, probably woven by Uzbeks in urban centers such as Bukhara, were the source of similar designs used by the Ersari.

PLATE 66 (ABOVE LEFT).
Ersari carpet (fragment).
Worn pile. Both rugs
photographed from back.

PLATE 67 (ABOVE RIGHT).
Ersari carpet (fragment)
(detail). Worn pile. Both rugs
photographed from back.

two-rib selvages in the same wool that is used in the body of the rug. The outer guard stripe of these pieces is, however, common on gul rugs. One may occasionally even find a rug in an ikat-derived design with a structure suggesting an Uzbek or Kazak origin.

The Kizil Ayak

The Kizil Ayak are another group of uncertain affinity; when the term Kizil Ayak is used in Afghanistan, it is applied to part of the Ersari-related complex. Moshkova[80] described them as differing in appearance from the Ersari and resembling more the Tekke, reporting that they saw themselves as related to the Merv Tekkes.

Bogolyubov illustrated two rugs that he labeled as Kizil Ayaks.[81] Both show some similarities to the rug in plate 68 of this catalogue, but the resemblance is not close enough to establish that they are made by the same group. In plate 26 of his text, Bogolyubov illustrates a rug in which there is only one animal figure in each quadrant of a rounded *göl;* in the Wiedersperg rug we see two animal figures per quadrant in a much flatter *göl* on a rug that, although of a similar size to the Ersari gul rugs he describes, is of so different a texture that it may hardly be described as the same type; it differs even more markedly from the Beshir type. To all appearances, it fits well into the group of rugs currently being labeled Kizil Ayak.

Perceptions of what constitutes a Kizil Ayak weaving seem to have changed. In 1969 Schürmann labeled as a Kizil Ayak an ensi that,

PLATE 68. Kizil Ayak main carpet

PLATE 69. Kizil Ayak or
Ersari bag *(chuval)*

coincidentally, is currently part of the Wiedersperg Collection (see pl. 7) and is now attributed to the Saryk.[82] It has also become fashionable of late to label the bags with the design shown in plate 69 as Kizil Ayak work, and this is at least plausible. Such pieces have neither a Beshir weave nor one similar to the Ersari gul rugs. Late versions of this design appeared regularly in the Kabul bazaar during the 1970s, and they show a structure consistent with larger rugs called Kizil Ayak.

The larger rugs with the *tauk nuska göl* seldom have more than between 110 and 120 knots to the square inch; some chuvals that have recently been ascribed to the Kizil Ayak have double this number or more. Although they are asymmetrically knotted, these chuvals are clearly not Tekke or Salor, nor, because of their asymmetrical knotting, can they be Saryk, in spite of traces of silk in some examples and similarities in design. For such reasons the Kizil Ayak label has yet to be clearly defined. A good example of this bag type, although not among the most finely knotted, is illustrated in plate 69. It is also possible that the bag was made by a weaver from a tribal group that was originally part of the Saryk, then merged with the Kizil Ayak in Afghanistan.[83]

The Beshir Rug

Whether one calls these rugs Beshir, after the town just east of the middle Amu Darya, or Beshiri, which suggests a tribal origin—the name one encounters when these rugs appear in Afghanistan—the label is hardly precise, although it has stuck fairly consistently since Bogolyubov used it in 1908.[84] This is the type most frequently associated with designs that are not part of the Turkmen tradition and dimensions that appear to have nothing to do with nomadic life. Beshir rugs twenty feet in length were surely made for urban use, and the thirty-one-foot *saf* (the largest Beshir piece known to the authors) was almost certainly woven for a mosque.[85] Indeed, the dimensions of many of these pieces, which may be twice as long—or more—as they are wide, suggest those of large Persian rugs from the middle of the last third of the nineteenth century, when rugs specifically sized for Western rooms started to flow from the looms. Surely some survivors of this type date from early periods, and many show designs clearly adapted from Persian sources. The Herati pattern is common, along with the mîna khâni and various repeating floral designs derived from nineteenth-century Persian types.[86] Medallion rugs are known, although the medallions themselves are often smaller and simpler than one would find on a Persian rug of the same size. Compartment designs (see pl. 74), stylized "cloud bands" (see pls. 70–72), repeating *boteh* figures, and other staples of the Persian repertoire are also found in a variety of sizes. With the possible exception of rather large chuvals, however, there are few examples of the woven trappings associated with nomadic life in any of these design types. There is substantial historical evidence that rugs in these styles were woven in towns.

Moshkova is specific about the towns and villages involved, and we have no reason to doubt her assertion that these rugs were produced in Beshir, Burdalyk, and Chakyr, and in other parts of the Khojambas, Khalaj, and Burdalyk regions.[87] Moshkova gives reason for believing that these areas may well have produced carpets described in fifth- to seventh-century Chinese sources, which made detailed references to carpets being woven in sites that are now thought to represent Karshi and possibly Beshir.[88] In addition she cites Arab geographers who mention rug weaving in and around Bukhara from the seventh through the eleventh centuries, an occupation almost certainly associated with the area's indigenous Iranian population.

Perhaps the most surprising data produced by Moshkova concerns the composition of the local populations in this region. She notes that Salors and Olams made up the largest part of the population, with Ersaris a distinct minority. The former had, apparently, entirely abandoned their traditional designs and were weaving rugs of the local type. The Olams are of controversial origin, but the best available information suggests that, rather than Turkmen, they are a remnant population of the indigenous Iranian people,[89] quite possibly descendants of the Alans, a Sarmatian tribe, elements of which swept through Europe in the fifth century, settling as far west as northern France (Alençon) and Spain (the name Catalonia is probably derived from Goth-Alania). That the Olam had a major part in the production of Beshir-type rugs raises several interesting possibilities pertaining to the presence of Persian designs in this region, but this probably relates more to this area's being closer to the Persian trading sphere than it does to any kind of cultural continuity. It may help explain, however, why the weavings from this region show less in the way of Turkmen design traditions than do those made in areas where a substantial majority of the population is Turkmen.

As for the rugs themselves, they are limp, like the typical Ersari gul rug, although some later pieces are firmer. Essentially all are asymmetrically knotted, with the knot open to the right or, less commonly, to the left; the warps seldom show substantial depression, although some pieces are slightly ribbed. Knot density ranges from between about forty and eighty per square inch, and the double weft is standard. Edge and end finishes differ from those of the Ersari gul rugs, as there is far less use of the brown goat-hair selvage. Often there is a narrow two- or three-rib selvage made up of colors used within the rug, occasionally in a checkerboard pattern. The ends may show a plain-weave band, usually red with blue stripes, but it is ordinarily shorter than those on Ersari gul rugs.

Red remains a prominent color, but there are Beshir types with ivory or blue fields. One possible way of identifying an earlier generation of Beshir rugs is the presence of a field that varies in small irregular patches from dark blue to blue green, light blue, and brown. This is particularly well exemplified in the carpets illustrated in plates 70, 71, and 72, the last being only a fragment. It is not entirely clear why the design in these carpets has been given the label cloud band, the shape of which the repeating figures resemble, but there is also the possibility of a botanic or zoomorphic origin. The usual variation in field colors, along with frequent small, rounded patches of red, which are found on renditions of the Herati designs, may be seen in plates 70 and 71. Rugs made later are more likely to have a solid field color. Later rugs are also most likely to show wider main borders or more numerous border stripes. The red in the most recent seems weaker, tending to fade toward pink. This is true even in examples that are still dyed with madder, suggesting that by the early twentieth century less of the dye was used, perhaps because its price had risen.

This group of rugs does not ordinarily include the trappings of a nomadic lifestyle, but one does encounter some chuvals and large torbas—of the type called *jollars* in Afghanistan—that seem to have the structure and color scheme associated with the Beshir and use similar

PLATE 70. Beshir carpet

PLATE 71. Beshir carpet

PLATE 72. Beshir carpet (fragment). Worn pile. Photographed from back.

designs, often from Persian sources. At times figures from the Herati design are used, often without a recognizable version of the entire design, and there are a number of chuvals in the mina khani design, usually finer in weave than the typical Beshir object and occasionally containing small quantities of silk in the pile. Some examples of this design appear to be the work of unidentified Turkmen in Afghanistan. A few Beshir pieces reveal traces of a nomadic tradition, although the colors and designs of the nineteenth-century commercial Beshir rug predominate. For instance, an asmalyk that appeared at auction in 1998 was, in all respects, Beshir in style;[90] one may assume that it was woven by sedentary people for an earlier ceremonial tradition.

The carpet shown in plate 73 may be based upon the same source as the so-called Bakhtiari rugs, in which stylized floral figures appear in roughly square compartments. Note the lack of a goat-hair selvage

PLATE 73. Beshir carpet

and the guard stripes with a yellow ground, which are common on this type of Beshir. Several rugs showing lozenge-shaped forms within rectangular compartments (such as that in plate 74) are known, and usually they have a finer weave and a slightly lower pile than most Beshirs do. Here the compartments are more clearly delineated than they are in most rugs of the type.

BESHIR PRAYER-RUG DESIGNS

The first Beshir-type rugs to command high prices at auction, at the beginning of the great Turkmen rug enthusiasm of the 1970s, were a type of prayer rug that shows a weave typical of Ersari rugs, but with the edge and end finish of the Beshir. Many of the earliest also show the variation in the field color described above. These relatively narrow rugs often have a pomegranate design, usually with an archlike figure at the top, or with geometric figures arranged in broad vertical

PLATE 74. Beshir carpet

PLATE 75. Beshir prayer rug *(namazlyk)*

PLATE 76. Beshir wedding trapping *(asmalyk)*

bands. The rug shown in plate 75 is probably a late-nineteenth-century example, without the variation in the field color. A few of these rugs show an ivory field, and usually the borders are narrow. A small number of Beshir safs are known, including a particularly appealing example with a white field.[91]

BESHIR-TYPE BAGS AND TRAPPINGS

The boundary between bags and trappings in the Beshir style and that of the gul rugs is tenuous, and one cannot always clearly assign these smaller pieces to either category. Here we may actually be dealing with more than two types of weavings, and there seems to be little point in attempting to assign each example to a specific category. Probably because the mina khani design is a classic Persian type that could hardly be considered as having a tribal significance, and because large mina khani design rugs clearly of the Beshir type are known, chuvals of this design are often given the Beshir label. A careful inspection of some of these pieces, however, suggests that this may not always be accurate. Some are surprisingly fine and thus do not seem as likely to be Beshir rugs. Such pieces may also show patches of several colors of silk, including yellow, light blue, and pink, often of a thinner gauge yarn than the pile wool; there have been suggestions that it is the kind of silk used for embroideries. The asmalyk shown in plate 76 exhibits some features of color and structure that could quite plausibly place it in either the Beshir or the Ersari group. One should not be too dogmatic about this label.

The Karakalpak or Uzbek

There are two rugs in the Wiedersperg Collection with large *tauk nuska göl*s in which each quadrant shows a quadruped with a clearly delineated head and large tail. The *göl*s are octagons made up of straight lines, and the rugs have simple, geometric minor gul figures and relatively narrow borders. The tribal origin of rugs with this same basic design is still undetermined. The first example of this type to appear in print was published by Bogolyubov, who illustrated a quarter of a rug with a design similar to that of the carpet shown in plate 77, including essentially the same major border and the same outer minor border. In both rugs the animal figures are arranged so that their heads point toward the center of the gul. The Bogolyubov rug, which has apparently not survived, was purchased in the Samarkand bazaar and was described as being in poor condition even then. Bogolyubov found a new carpet of the same design and was informed that it had been woven in the Karakalpak village of Kara Abdal in the district of Jisak.[92] Another Karakalpak piece with a different design was also attributed to this area. (Soviet scholars have theorized that the Karakalpak were originally an Iranian tribe who adapted cultural characteristics of the Turkmen, living a sedentary, agricultural existence in the Amu Darya Delta and parts of the Nurata and Samarkand regions.)

The appearance of Moshkova's book in 1970 and its subsequent translation into German and English have provided yet further opinions on the origin of this particular gul. Having visited the Nurata region in 1944 and 1946, Moshkova concluded that rugs of this design were produced by the Turkmen Uzbeks, a people of probable Turkmen origin who had become assimilated into the cultural fabric of the Uzbeks among whom they lived. Moshkova found little trace of carpet weaving during her visit and concluded that Bogolyubov's attributions were incorrect.[93] Some authors, as a result, have recently begun labeling rugs of this design as work of the Turkmen Uzbeks of the Nurata region, but Bogolyubov presumably had specific information about where the rugs that he purchased were woven at a time when they were still being made.

There are indeed enough differences among rugs with this gul to suggest that it may have been used by more than one tribal group. A rug first published in 1973,[94] when compared side by side with that shown in plate 77, reveals an altogether different texture and substantial differences in structure. The Wiedersperg piece has deeply depressed alternate warps, suggestive of a Bijar; the other piece has warps all on the same level. The color tonalities, too, are substantially different.

The carpet illustrated in plate 78 has, however, a markedly different texture from either of the pieces in plates 76 and 77 and shows

PLATE 77. Karakalpak or Uzbek carpet

PLATE 78. Karakalpak or Uzbek carpet

the same major border as a rug published in the English edition of Moshkova's *Carpets of the People of Central Asia*.[95] Yet another, obviously recent piece with essentially the same gul, which was examined at the Museum of Fine Arts in Samarkand in 1995, was clearly similar in texture and color to contemporary rugs known to be from the Turkmen Uzbeks of the Nurata area, although it had nothing more than the gul in common with the carpet in plate 77. There may be more than one source of rugs showing this large gul with a quadruped in each quadrant, as they do not all seem to have the same structural characteristics. In deciding who was most likely to have obtained accurate on-the-spot information, Bogolyubov or Moshkova, one may entertain a slight preference for Bogolyubov, as his investigations occurred while such rugs were, one may suppose, still being woven. This likelihood falls short, nevertheless, of being a conclusive means of identifying the whole group of rugs with this gul, although it seems to rule out a Turkmen source.

Palas (Flatwoven Rugs)

The term *palas* in Central Asia and the Caucasus refers to flatweaves and includes both plainwoven textiles and brocades. Because the Turkmen palas was often large and not very colorful, few early collectors or dealers brought them to the West, and even now they are ignored by most collectors and neglected by scholars. No attempt has yet been made either to study the relatively few Turkmen palas designs or to define any differences among the structures in the supplementary weft brocading technique employed. Consequently, there is little evidence on which to base datings or attributions to particular Turkmen tribes.

Three different experts on Turkmen rugs have published flatweaves with the design of that in plate 79 as Tekke (evidence sufficient for the Red Queen).[96] The rug can be read in two ways. In one, the design consists of large red diamonds overlapping one other along their vertical and horizontal axes, with small blue diamonds at the vertical intersections and with larger, quartered diamonds of blue and white along the horizontal. In the second interpretation, the eye sees the design as a series of repeating double-kochak motifs, the interstices of which are occupied by the small blue or the blue and white diamonds. In both cases, when the rug is viewed at even a short distance, the individual design elements dissolve into an overall pattern of light and dark vertical stripes as a result of the alignment of the two sets of smaller diamonds.

An equally complex design patterns the palas in plate 80, of Tekke or perhaps Yomut origin. Difficult to read because of its density and its small scale, the design is composed of a dark blue diamond lattice

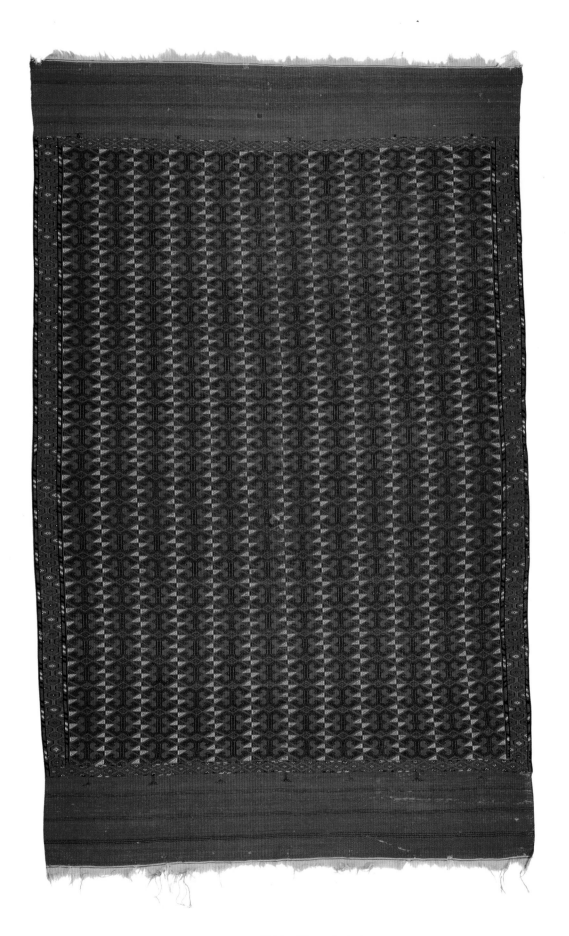

PLATE 79. Tekke (?) rug (*palas*)

PLATE 80. Tekke or Yomut rug (*palas*)

PLATE 81. Baluch prayer rug *(namazlyk)*

with a modified kochak-cross motif at the center of each compartment and red diamonds at the points where the compartments intersect. Short white and light red lines in the spaces between adjacent kochaks intersect with the white centers of the compartments to form a secondary diamond lattice system.

Such designs reward an observer who is willing to spend time with them. Other examples in the literature that vary in detail and complexity have been attributed to both the Tekke and the Yomut.[97]

PLATE 79 (ABOVE LEFT, DETAIL).
Tekke rug *(palas)*

PLATE 80 (ABOVE RIGHT, DETAIL).
Tekke or Yomut rug *(palas)*

A Baluch Rug

The prayer rug shown in plate 81 is of no specifically identifiable group, although it is considered to be a Baluchi type. It is interesting in that it shows three mihrab-like elements across the top that are strongly suggestive of those found on many Beshir-type prayer rugs. It is not uncommon to find such rugs with designs adapted from the Turkmen.

REFERENCES

1. The Sasanians were the ruling dynasty of Iran from the third to the seventh centuries; the Sogdians were an Iranian people whose territory, Sogdania, was roughly equivalent to today's Uzbekistan and Tajikistan.

2. V. G. Moshkova, "Tribal Göls on Turkoman Carpets," 16–26 in *Turkoman Studies* 1, ed. R. Pinner and M. Franses (London: Oguz Press, 1980); trans. from *Sovietskaya Etnografiya* (1946): 145–62.

3. Moshkova's Cyrillic term may be transliterated as *tovuk musga* (from the Turkish *tavuk* meaning "hen" and *muska* meaning "amulet"). It has been thought that *tavuk* is corrupted from *tavus* ("peacock"), an avatar for the "Great Bird," and a more appropriate symbol than the mere domestic hen; see R. Pinner, *The Rickmers Collection—Turkoman Rugs* (Berlin: Staatliche Museen zu Berlin, 1993), 18–19.

4. Moshkova (in "Tribal Göls") was the first to suggest a totemic function, and in the same publication, a hypothesis about the existence of "living" and "dead" *göls.*

5. L. Mackie and J. Thompson, *Turkmen Tribal Rugs and Traditions* (Washington, D.C.: Textile Museum, 1980), plate 62.

6. D. Dodds and M. Eiland, eds., *Oriental Rugs from Atlantic Collections* (Philadelphia, Pa.: International Conference on Oriental Carpets, 1966), plate 180.

7. These results were reported at a symposium held in Basel, Switzerland, in February 1999; they have not yet been published. Among the objects tested was the Tekke torba published in P. Hoffmeister and A. S. B. Crosby, *Turkomen Carpets in Franconia* (Edinburgh: Crosby Press, 1980), plate 25.

8. V. V. Barthold, *Four Studies on the History of Central Asia,* vol. 3, trans. V. and T. Minorsky (Leiden: E. J. Brill, 1962), 75–170.

9. F. Sümer, A. E. Uysal, and W. S. Walker, trans. and ed., *The Book of Dede Korkut* (Austin, Tex.: University of Texas Press, 1972).

10. Barthold, *Four Studies.*

11. Ibid., 132.

12. Ibid., citing Iskander-Munshi, 147–48.

13. Ibid., 169.

14. First naming them S-group carpets, Jon Thompson subsequently identified the carpets with the Salor; see A. A. Bogolyubov, *Carpets of Central Asia,* trans. and ed. Jon Thompson (Basingstoke, England: Crosby Press, 1973).

15. The exception would be the few smaller and less finely woven carpets, as exemplified by possibly the earliest of the known Salor main carpets, which differs from others by having the *chemche gül* as the secondary ornament; see R. Pinner, *Antique Carpets from Austrian Collections* (Vienna: Society for Textile Art Research, 1986), plate 101.

16. A smaller version of this secondary *gül* is used on Yomut chuvals; see, for example, plate 39 in this catalogue.

17. The kochanak border appears in the same form on a number of fifteenth-century Turkish carpets, including both small- and large-pattern Holbein carpets. Simplified versions of this border are seen on examples from other Turkmen tribes as well as on later Turkish and Caucasian carpets.

18. R. Neugebauer and J. Orendi, *Orientalische Teppichkunde* (Vienna: Hiersemann, 1908), plate 14.

19. U. Schürmann, *Central Asian Rugs* (Frankfurt am Main: Osterrieth, 1969), plate 7.

20. For an account of the traditional Turkmen wedding ritual, see R. Pinner, "The Turkmen Wedding," *Hali,* no. 100 (1998): 104–107.

21. Moshkova reports that the term *kejebe,* which is derived from the Persian for camel-flank panniers, was adopted by the Turkmen for the bride's palanquin on the wedding camel; see V. G. Moshkova, *Die Teppiche de Volker Mittelasiens im späten ixi und xx Jahrhundert* (Hamburg: Reinhold Schletzer Verlag, 1970); idem, *Carpets of the People of Central Asia,* trans. and ed. George O'Bannon and Ovadan Amanova-Olsen (Tucson, Ariz., n.p., 1996); originally in Russian, published in Tashkent, 1970.

22. It is apparent that the Wiedersperg trapping, like several others, originally possessed a shoulder on each side, to which fringes were attached for extra decoration.

23. W. Wood, "Turkmen Ethnohistory," in *Vanishing Jewels: Central Asian Tribal Weavings,* ed. George W. O'Bannon et al., exh. cat. (Rochester, N.Y.: Rochester Museum and Science Center, 1990), 33.

24. Barthold, *Four Studies,* 169; citing C. E. Yate, *Northern Afghanistan* (1888), 189.

25. Moshkova (*Teppiche de Volker Mittelasiens,* p. 21, fig. 35) referred to this ornament as the *temirjin göl,* a term followed by authors in the West. She also describes

it as an *onurga göl,* translated as "backbone" and a name employed by several Turkmen and Russian authors, among them A. N. Pirkuliyeva, *Kovrovoi tkaktschestrva turkmen dolino srednii Amu-Dari* (Moscow: USSR Academy of Science, 1966). This appears incorrect, as the Turkish for backbone is *omurga,* which we have used in this catalogue. Although there is no Turkish word *onurga,* its root, *onur,* means "honor," "pride," or "self-respect," sentiments not inappropriate for a tribal *göl. Onurga* may not, therefore, be a mistake but a calque, containing the meanings of both words.

26. The term *gülli göl* (flower or rose *göl*) is in common use in the West. The equally appropriate *gushly göl* (bird *göl*) is used in Turkmenistan.

27. Forms of the Memling gul (the ornament appears in Turkish carpets in two paintings by the fifteenth-century Netherlandish artist Hans Memling) appear in a wide variety of carpets from Turkey and throughout central Asia. See, for example, Pinner, *Rickmers Collection,* plate 2.

28. "The Khan's Kibitka," *Illustrated London News,* 28 March 1985, 318.

29. Schürmann, *Central Asian Rugs,* plate 36.

30. For similar Saryk torbas, see J. Cassin and P. Hoffmeister (1988), plate 7; Tzareva (1984), plate 20; Pinner, *Rickmers Collection*; and M. L. Eiland, ed., *Oriental Rugs from Pacific Collections* (San Francisco: 1990), plate 137.

31. Barthold, *Four Studies,* 133; citing Abul-Ghazi, *Histoire des Mogols et des Tartares,* trans. and annotated Baron Desmaison (1871–1874).

32. Barthold, *Four Studies,* 147, 151, 150, 164.

33. Wood, "Turkmen Ethnohistory," 30.

34. Barthold, *Four Studies,* 166.

35. Halil Inalcik, *The Ottoman Empire: The Classical Age, 1300–1600* (London: 1973), 6ff.

36. Rudi Paul Linder, *Nomads and Ottomans in Medieval Anatolia,* Uralic and Altai Series, vol. 144 (Bloomington, Ind.: Indiana University), 107, 109.

37. R. Pinner and M. Franses, "The Animal-Tree *Ensi,"* in *Turkoman Studies* 1, ed. R. Pinner and M. Franses (London: Oguz Press, 1980).

38. For *ayna* gul chuvals, see R. Pinner and L. Pinner in *Turkmen Tribal Rugs and Traditions,* ed. L. Mackie and J. Thompson (Washington, D.C.: Textile Museum, 1980), 203–15.

39. A. A. Felkerzam, *Alte Teppiche Mittelasiens* (Hamburg: 1979) (originally published in *Starye Gody* [Saint Petersburg], June 1914, 57–133; October 1915, 17–40); Moshkova, *Teppiche de Volker Mittelasiens,* fig. 93; S. M. Dudin, "Kovrovye izdeliya Srednej Azii," *Sbornik Muzeya Antropologii i Etnografii* 7 (Leningrad) (1928): 71–155; idem, "Teppiche Mittelasiens," in *Turkmenenforschung* 5 (Hamburg) (1984).

40. P. A. Andrews, "The Turkmen Tent," in *Turkmen Tribal Rugs and Traditions,* ed. L. Mackie and J. Thompson (Washington, D.C.: Textile Museum, 1980).

41. Other pieces of this type have been published in C. D. Reed, *Turkoman Rugs* (Cambridge, Mass.: Fogg Art Museum,1966); E. Herrmann, *Von Uschak bis Yarkand* (Munich: n.d.), plate 90; W. Loges, *Turkoman Tribal Carpets,* trans. Raoul Tschebull (London: Allen and Unwin, 1980), plate 11.

42. S. Azadi, *Wie Blumen in der Wüste,* exh. cat. (Hamburg: International Conference on Oriental Carpets, 1993).

43. The curled-leaf design is used in some early ensis on the two outer borders, to make a shape that would match the arms of the kapunuk.

44. In a few door surrounds known from the Yomut and associated tribes, the arms are shorter in relation to the length.

45. Since Pinner and Franses listed six known examples of the animal-tree asmalyk *(see* R. Pinner and M. Franses, "The Bird and Animal-Tree Asmalyk," in

Turkoman Studies 1, ed. R. Pinner and M. Franses [London: Oguz Press, 1980]), three more have been discovered, including the fine example illustrated in plate 25 of this catalogue.

46. Moshkova gives *ak yüp* and *yolam* as the names used for these tent bands, the latter name possibly from the Turkish *kolan,* meaning "girth" or "belt." See Moshkova, *Carpets of the People,* 47, 54.

47. Bogolyubov, *Carpets of Central Asia,* plate 13.

48. A. Rautenstengel and V. Rautenstengel, "Turkmen Main Carpets of Different Tribes with 'Eagle' and *Dyrnak Göls:* A Comparison of Their Structure and Their Decoration" (in German), in A. Rautenstengel, V. Rautenstengel, and S. Azadi, *Studien zur Teppich-Kultur der Turkmen* (Hilden, Germany: 1990).

49. S. Azadi, "Göklan Turkmen and Their Carpets," 120–47 in *Oriental Carpet and Textile Studies,* vol. 3, 1989.

50. A. Rautenstengel, V. Rautenstengel, and S. Azadi, *Studien zur Teppich-Kultur der Turkmen* (Hilden, Germany: 1990), plate 20.

51. The "running-dog" border consists of reciprocal waves woven in two alternating colors.

52. Barthold, *Four Studies,* 160–65.

53. Ibid., 168.

54. Cited in Tadeuz Mankowski, "Some Documents from Polish Sources Relating to Carpet Making in the Time of Shah Abbas," pp. 2431–36 in *A Survey of Persian Art,* ed. A. U. Pope and P. Ackerman (London: Oxford University Press, 1938–39).

55. Barthold, *Four Studies,* 146–61.

56. Mankowski, "Some Documents," 2431.

57. There are many forms of Persian palmette, and one should not expect to find an exact correspondence between the versions that came into use in the Caucasus and those that were found in parts of the Persian sphere inhabited by Turkmen. The eagle gul appears to have been derived from the same forms as the "flaming palmettes" found on a number of eighteenth-century Caucasian rugs (e.g., Kirchheim, *Orient Stars* [Stuttgart: Heinrich Kircheim; London: Hali Publications, 1993], plate 78; and C. G. Ellis, *Early Caucasian Rugs* [Washington, D.C.: Textile Museum, 1975], plate 30, which also shows small six-sided figures with hooks that could be analogous to *kepse* guls). The Turkmen form developed from a horizontally symmetrical shape to one that is wider at one end than at the other. The gul-like figure on the Hecksher rug (Dodds and Eiland, eds., *Oriental Rugs from Atlantic Collections,* plate 180) was surely based upon the kinds of palmettes that may be seen on the so-called "shield carpets" from the Caucasus (R. Pinner and M. Franses, "Caucasian Shield Carpets," *Hali* 1, no. 1 [1978]: 4–22).

58. Mackie and Thompson, *Turkmen Tribal Rugs,* 150 and plate 62; Schürmann, *Central Asian Rugs,* plate 23; Dodds and Eiland, eds., *Oriental Rugs from Atlantic Collections,* fig. 180.

59. Mackie and Thompson, *Turkmen Tribal Rugs,* 146–48.

60. The carpet has been tested twice. The results of the first test, reported 15 Feb. 1996 by the Rafter Radiocarbon Laboratory, New Zealand, showed an interval of 1427 to 1642 A.D. with 95% confidence. The second, issued 3 Feb. 1997 in Zurich, indicated an interval of 1487 to 1894 with 95% confidence.

61. Rautenstengel, Rautenstengel, and Azadi, *Studien zur Teppich-Kultur.*

62. H. Sienknecht, "The Development of Ornament on Yomut C-gul Carpets," *Hali* 11, no. 47 (October 1989): 30–39.

63. Ibid., 38–39.

64. R. Pinner, "Fragments," *Hali* 17, no. 84 (1996): 63.

65. Bogolyubov, *Carpets of Central Asia,* plate 23.

66. Moshkova, *Carpets of the People,* 257–60.

67. Ibid., 257.

68. Dodds and Eiland, eds., *Oriental Rugs from Atlantic Collections,* 172.

69. Ibid., 201.

70. K. Muncacsi, "Dividing the Chaudor," *Hali* 77 (1994): 96–107.

71. Moshkova, *Carpets of the People,* 276.

72. The best known is an ensi in the König Collection in Switzerland; see M. Rothberg, "Arabachi," *Hali* no. 96 (1998), 97, fig. 11, which appears opposite the Wiedersperg Arabachi ensi illustrated in figure 10.

73. In Moshkova, *Carpets of the People,* 298–99.

74. Bogolyubov, *Carpets of Central Asia,* plate 24.

75. Barthold, *Four Studies,* 137.

76. Moshkova, *Carpets of the People,* 269.

77. Barthold citing Abul Ghazi, *Four Studies,* 151; Bogolyubov, *Carpets of Central Asia,* 21; G. Jarring, *On the Distribution of Turk Tribes in Afghanistan* (Lund, Sweden: Gleerup, 1938).

78. Eiland, *Oriental Rugs from Pacific Collections,* 121–23.

79. G. O'Bannon, "The Saltiq Ersari Carpet," *Afghanistan,* no. 3 (1977): 111–21.

80. Moshkova, *Carpets of the People,* 269.

81. Bogolyubov, *Carpets of Central Asia,* plates 25, 26.

82. Schürmann, *Central Asian Rugs,* plate 36.

83. For an illustration of a type of chuval that is considered by Western collectors to be Kizil Ayak work, see Loges, *Turkoman Tribal Rugs,* plate 75.

84. Bogolyubov, *Carpets of Central Asia,* plate 28.

85. M. L. Eiland, *Oriental Rugs: A New Comprehensive Guide* (Boston: Little Brown, 1981), plate 30.

86. R. Pinner, "The Beshir Carpets of the Bukhara Emirate," *Hali* 3, no. 4 (1981): 294–304.

87. Moshkova, *Carpets of the People,* 300–303.

88. Ibid., 8–9.

89. Ibid., 269–70.

90. Rippon Boswell, Wiesbaden, 23 May 1988, lot 95.

91. Moshkova, *Carpets of the People.* The ivory-field saf is depicted on the cover.

92. Bogolyubov, *Carpets of Central Asia,* plate 29.

93. Moshkova, *Carpets of the People,* 106–21.

94. Eiland, *Oriental Rugs,* plate 26.

95. Moshkova, *Carpets of the People,* plate 49.

96. Similar palas have been illustrated by Bogolyubov, *Carpets of Central Asia,* plate 45; W. Grote-Hasenbalg, *Der Orientteppich,* vol. 1 (Berlin: Scarabaeus, 1922), plate XVI; H. McCoy Jones and J. W. Boucher, *Rugs of the Yomud Tribes* (Washington, D.C.: International Hajji Baba Society, 1970), no. 124; *Turkmen Szonyegek* (Miscolc, 1979), no. 32; H. Bausback, *The Old and Antique Oriental Art of Weaving* (in German) (Mannheim: 1982), 135; Lefevre, London, 29 May 1981, lot 28; P. Ramsey, "Flatweaves of Central Asia," *Oriental Carpet and Textile Studies,* vol. 1 (London: 1985), fig. 1; Pinner, *Antique Carpets from Austrian Collections,* plate 123.

97. For simpler and variant examples of flatwoven carpets and tent bags, see Bogolyubov, *Carpets of Central Asia,* plate 44; A. N. Landreau and W. R. Pickering, *From the Bosporus to Samarkand: Flat Woven Rugs* (Washington, D.C.: Textile Museum, 1966), plate 73; A. B. Tacher, *Turkoman Rugs* (New York: Weyhe, 1949), plate 54; J. Straka and Louise M. Mackie, *The Oriental Rug Collection of Jerome and Mary Jane Straka* (New York: 1978), plate 52; Pinner, *Rickmers Collection,* plate 57.

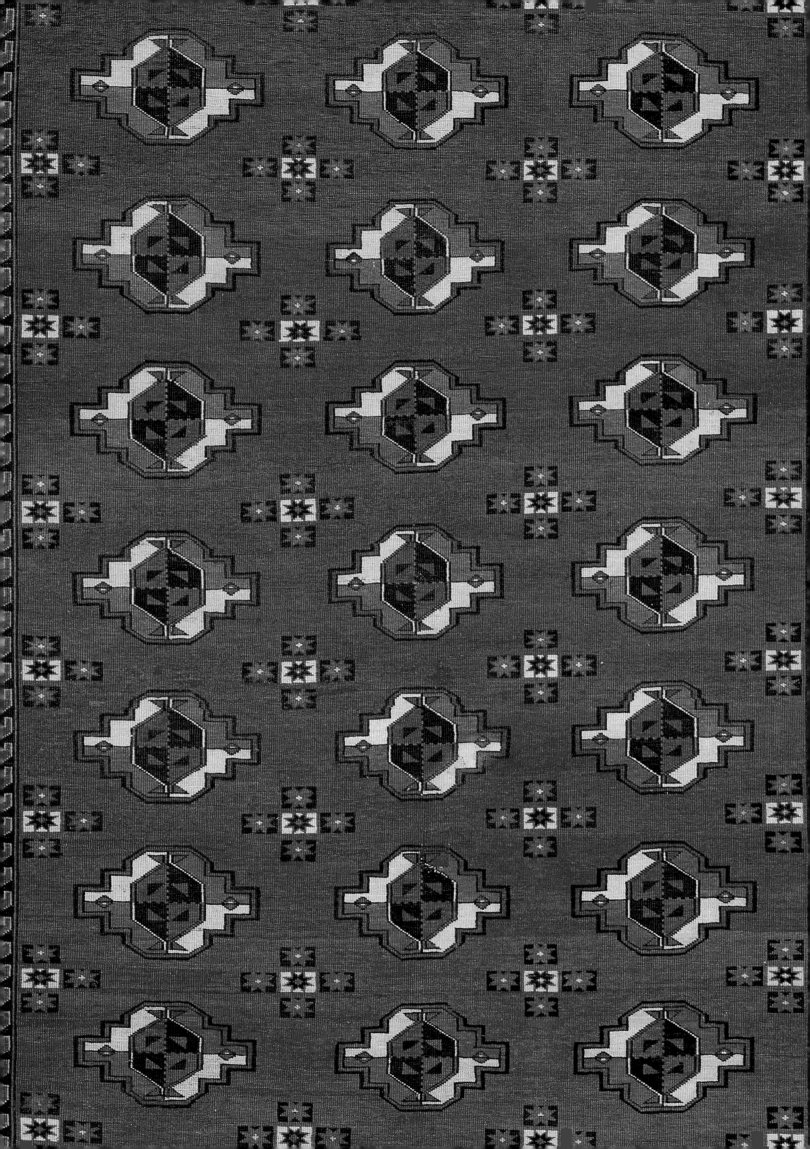

Notes on the

Structural Analysis

of Turkmen Rugs

Murray L. Eiland, Jr.

Ordinarily the Turkmen rug presents few challenges to those who do structural analyses, but problems of interpretation do arise and several issues elicit differing solutions. The structural analyses in this catalogue should be read with the following caveats in mind.

WARP. The warp is ostensibly the simplest part of the rug to describe, as it is virtually always wool and made up of two Z-spun singles plied in the S-direction (Z2S). It is the color and composition that may become problematic. One often finds warps (as well as wefts and edge finishes) described as goat hair, but this should be taken as being somewhat imprecise. The wool from many sheep is composed of coarse fibers with a large component of hair, and there are even ways of separating out the hair—the straighter, coarser fibers—from the finer wool fibers. One still cannot be certain that much of what is customarily described as goat hair is not actually from sheep. At times warps are made from singles, each of a different undyed color, plied together. Even less certain is the identification of camel hair, which is difficult even with a microscope. The scale pattern differs slightly from that of sheep's wool, as does the percentage of medullated fibers, and camel hair may contain pigment granules visible with moderate magnification. Use of this term without such an examination may be misleading.

There is also some question regarding color. Many of the warps in Turkmen rugs are one shade or another of brown; for example, gray brown is common in Ersari rugs and a light brown more common in Tekkes. The problem with light brown is that, where the yarn had

Turkman wedding procession, 1924.
The bride is seated within an elaborately decorated, domed camel saddle.
Its lightweight struts are topped with a cover of white felt with applied designs and
ornaments, and the exterior is hung with various types of small carpets and bags.

unwound in the fringe, it may appear to be ivory while it still appears light brown in the body of the rug. During the spinning and plying of the low-grade wool and hair used in warps, there is a natural variation in color along the length of the strand, and one may find all sorts of variation from light to dark in the fringe. This does not necessarily mean that two distinct types of wool were used, only that there is much variation within the same batch of yarn.

WEFT. The sequence and make-up of rug wefts is more complex. In general, one could say that virtually all Turkmen rugs have two weft shots between rows of knots. Exceptions to this are extrafine Tekkes and later commercial Tekkes that may have been woven in the Merv Oasis, both of which sometimes have only one weft passage between rows. The fine pile tent bands also usually show one weft between the rows of knots.

Wool or goat hair is not always the only material used in wefts. Cotton (usually two-ply like the wool wefts) is often used and always undyed. Cotton appears most frequently in Chodor carpets, some having cotton wefts in most of the rug, others a combination of wool and cotton, i.e., sections in which the weft is entirely cotton and sections in which it is wool. There may be other areas of the rug in which the weft is made up of wool and cotton singles, but one does not encounter wefts in which cotton and wool are plied. Some rugs of the eagle gul group I type combine one yarn of cotton with another of silk.

Wool wefts are sometimes made up of yarns of different colors but, again, this is usually only because wool, even from the same sheep, often varies in color from one area to the next. Rarely, in Salor pieces, the weft is made up of two red or two pink yarns, and in some instances, only one of the yarns is red. Ordinarily, however, wefts in Turkmen rugs are not dyed.

Often the wefts may appear completely unplied for several inches before they can be seen to twist together. Whether such wefts should be described as lightly S-plied or as unplied is open to question. What has been observed is that two single strands of yarn may be wound together on a ball and not deliberately plied, but they twist together in such a manner as to give the appearance of being lightly plied. The way that this is reported in an analysis is a matter of personal preference, the terms *lightly plied* and *unplied* are both used. This begs the issue of how the wefts came to be as they are seen to be. At times such wefts are described as Z2 rather than as Z2S.

Most Persian, Turkish, and Caucasian rugs show distinctly different warps and wefts. Many Turkmen rugs seem to be made up of warps and wefts that are of the same material, the same spin and ply, and roughly the same thickness.

PILE. There is seldom any question about the identity of the knot in Turkmen rugs. Saryk rugs, particularly those thought to be earlier, are ordinarily symmetrically knotted, as are most Yomut rugs. This is more common on main carpets than on bag faces. Occasionally one will find a rug that appears to be an Ersari with symmetrical knots, but usually these are types that could have been woven by Uzbek groups. Almost all rugs identifiable as Ersari or Beshir are asymmetrically knotted, as are Salor, Tekke, Chodor, Arabachi, and eagle gul carpets.

Asymmetrical knots that are open to the left have been associated with the Salor (although perhaps 30 percent of their weavings have knots open to the right), the Arabachi, and eagle *gul* group I rugs. Tekke knots are traditionally open to the right, as are Chodor and most Ersari. Occasionally Ersari knots open to the left, and it is tempting to speculate that there may be some relationship between Ersari and Salor pieces, particularly if the designs appear related, as they sometimes do.

Tekke and asymmetrically knotted Yomut rugs frequently have symmetrical knots at the edges of rows of knots, which improves the stability of the pile. Edge knots on symmetrically knotted Yomut rugs were first identified by Beattie,[1] and another kind of edge knot was found by Azadi.[2] The former has been found on recent Yomut rugs from Iran; the latter appears on a Tekke chuval in the Rickmers Collection. No unusual edge knots were found on the rugs catalogued here.

Rug analyses often describe the degree to which alternate warps are depressed, but often in terms that are imprecise. Here we use only the descriptions slightly, moderately, or deeply depressed, rather than expressing the extent of the depression in degrees. It is not unusual for warps to be somewhat more deeply depressed in some parts of the rug than they are in others.

Pile yarns are almost always of two unplied wool yarns, although some insect-dyed yarn (cochineal or lac) may be exceptions. The pile yarns can be described as either unplied or lightly plied. Cotton and silk—which tend to be used in small patches—are ordinarily two-ply, although some silk have more plies. Some multi-plied silk yarns may have been intended for embroidery. White, particularly that found on some flatweaves, may also be plied of six or more strands, and this is likely to be machine spun.

Recently some pile yarns on eagle *gul* groups I and III rugs and insect-dyed yarns on other rugs have been found to be three-ply, and there have been reports of four-ply yarns. The number of plies in the knot yarns is easiest to see either at the base of the knots or on the back of the rug, but usually requires some magnification. In the eagle gul group III rug in the Wiedersperg Collection (see pl. 29) all of the yarns but the dark brown were observed to be composed of three singles. One of the Chodor rugs (see pl. 50) was also found to have some pile yarns with a make-up of three singles.

A legal assembly of the *majlis*, a convocation of Turkman elders, about 1920.
All the participants are seated on Turkman carpets. The most distinguished persons
are seated on the dais, on pile carpets that include a Turkman *ensi*. Labidjar
kilims cover the foreground, an area for persons of lesser rank.

Pile height is not included in these analyses as there were only a few places on a small percentage of the rugs in which the authors believed that the pile might approximate its original height. This information is seldom of diagnostic value.

SELVAGE FINISHES. Examination of an edge finish (or selvage) requires, first, that one determine whether it is original or was added to the rug later. There are rugs that show repair to the original finish, but so often on older rugs one finds a structure that is clearly recent or false selvages that have been sewn along the usually cut edges of a rug to stabilize them, preventing further damage. Instead of speculating about whether the new edge finish is simply a replacement of the original or an entirely different type of finish, the authors here have described it as having "no original selvage."

The simplest selvage finish on Turkmen rugs is a wool overcasting of several terminal warps, the number varying. Many Tekke carpets show a simple overcast, often in dark blue wool. One should check carefully to make certain that there are no modern, machine-spun wools used here, as this suggests that the structure is not original.

Selvages of two or more ribs (a term used here to refer to bundles of warps) appear on many Turkmen weavings, particularly those of the Ersari. Occasionally one will find a selvage made up exclusively of warps and wefts in what we describe as a plain interlaced selvage (with knotting). Usually, however, this is reinforced with additional yarns in what we label a reinforced selvage. In some Ersari rugs the reinforcing is the kind of brown or black hair usually described as goat hair, although it may be sheep's wool as well. The carpet illustrated in plate 55 has the widest reinforced selvage, with six ribs, each consisting of three warps.

Sometimes the reinforcing yarns interlace with the bundles of warps, giving stability to the structure. Some stability is also often provided by wefts that extend as far as the terminal warp or warp bundle. Rarely these reinforced selvages are made with yarns of several colors to form simple geometric designs, which we describe as checkerboard selvages.

Asmalyks and various other small trappings are often decorated with a variety of tassels and even braided bands. As with other types of edge finish, it is important to identify those structures that are not part of the original fabric.

END FINISHES. Original end finishes, like those of the selvages, are often missing, but here there is less likelihood that something entirely artificial will be added. Bands of weft-faced plain weave with weft yarns dyed in an approximation of the field color are most common, and rugs of the Tekke, Salor, and Saryk show many similarities. The main carpets often have a wide plain-weave band in red, with three groups of three blue stripes; occasionally this entire band is in knotted pile. In the few cases where the band is completely intact, there may be some terminal rows of ivory plain weave.

Tekke, Salor, and Saryk bags are most likely to show nothing more along the bottom than weft-faced plain weave in the field color, but at the top, this flatwoven band may have one or more blue stripes and the proximal portion is likely to be ivory. This is hemmed under. Yomut bags are usually finished in a similar manner, but the main carpets show several other features. The plain weave band at each end is seldom as wide as it is in Tekke, Salor, or Saryk carpets, but in the corners a number of warps are often left extra-long and often braided into a thick cord rope that may well have been used to suspend the rug. This braid seldom survives, but was probably originally present on some of the Yomut main carpets in this collection. At the base of the braid is a small, wedge-shaped prolongation of the kilim band, often with several narrow stripes. Ersari rugs with *guls* are more likely to show long kilim bands at the ends than are those with the Beshir label and designs from diverse, usually Persian, sources.

COLOR. Descriptions of color are likely to be imprecise, although the use of color plates perhaps makes this less important. The authors have resorted to the use of such analogies as comparisons to apricots and lemons, which may be misleading. But to give a simple color name, such as yellow, tells less than the full story, as the bright lemon yellow on many Tekkes and some Ersaris is quite different in quality from the pale, dull yellow on many Yomut main carpets. The deep green on some Saryks is also substantially different from the green, with pronounced abrash, found on some Ersaris, and the typical apricot on so many Tekkes becomes a much harsher tone on several types of Ersari weavings.

Description of the ground color of Yomut carpets is also challenging, with their multitude of gradations between purple, brown, and deep red. At times it is difficult to decide, for instance, whether "brownish purple" or "purplish brown" is more appropriate. Some version of Munsell's color chart may come into use in the future, but at present we must get by with descriptions that are, at best, approximations.

HANDLE AND TEXTURE. Information about handle and texture may be found in a number of recent structural analyses, but the authors have decided to omit it here because it does not seem to be diagnostically relevant to any object in this collection and, anyway, is often significantly dependent upon the degree to which a rug is worn.

REFERENCES

1. M. Beattie, "Pile and Flat-Weaves: Technical Notes," in Peter Andrews et al., *The Turcoman of Iran* (Kendal: Abbot Hall Art Gallery, 1971), 40.

2. S. Azadi, "Materials, Structures, and Related Features," in Pinner, *Rickmers Collection,* 83.

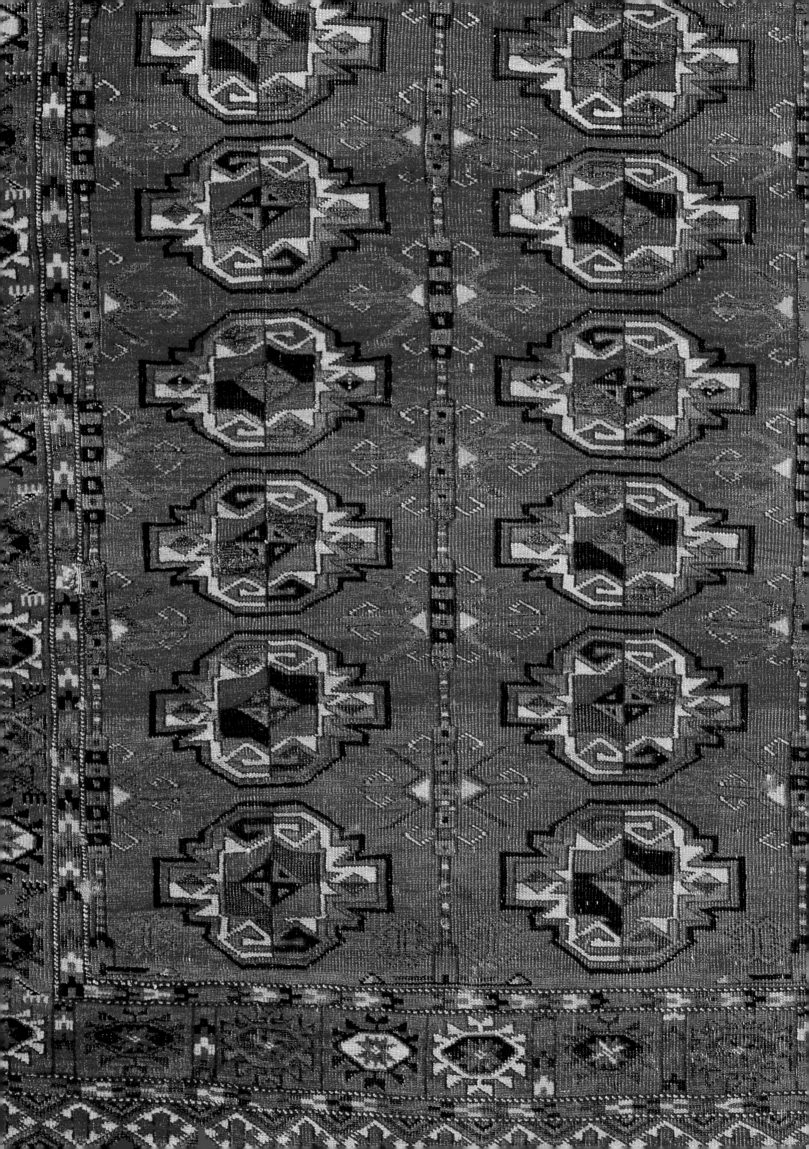

Structural Analyses

• *Turkmen bags (chuval, torba, etc.) are woven in one piece, the front continuous with the back. Because the backs are usually unpatterned and often damaged from use, dealers and collectors often cut them off to make the bag more decorative and easier to mount, as is the case in all of the bags in the Wiedersperg Collection. Catalogue entries such as "Salor bag" should therefore be understood to mean "Salor bag face"; the Turkmen terms apply to the bags in their complete form.*

• *The colors of the pile yarns are listed with the color of the field appearing first.*

• *Undyed yarns used for the warps and often the wefts of Turkmen carpets are usually made up of fibers that range from black or dark brown to white. Terms such as* ivory *or* dark brown *when applied to these yarns indicate the overall color impression that the yarns convey when seen from the distance of a approximately a foot or more.*

• *Dimensions are given with the height of the object, as it appears in the plate, first, followed by width.*

1. Salor main carpet

122 × 106 in. (310 × 269 cm)
WARP: wool, ivory to light brown, Z2S; alternate warps moderately depressed
WEFT: wool, ivory to light brown, 2Z; 2 shots
PILE: wool, 2Z; silk, Z2S
knot: asymmetrical, open on the left
count: 12–13 horiz. × 18 vert. per in. = 192–204 per sq. in.
colors: rust red, red brown, apricot, dark brown, dark blue, medium blue, light blue, ivory, magenta (silk only) (9)
SELVAGES: 6-rib reinforced selvage; red and blue wool reinforcing (Z2S)
ENDS: band of red weft-faced plain weave with two groups of three blue stripes (top and bottom)
1997.142.6

2. Salor bag *(chuval)*

32 × 48 in. (81 × 122 cm)
WARP: wool, light brown, Z2S; alternate warps slightly depressed
WEFT: wool, 2Z; 2 shots
PILE: wool, 2Z; silk, Z2S

knot: asymmetrical, open on the left
count: 14 horiz. × 18 vert. per in. = 252 per sq. in.
colors: brick red, red brown, dark blue, medium blue, magenta (silk only), brown, ivory (7)
SELVAGES: no original selvages
ENDS: band of ivory weft-faced plain weave, hemmed (top); narrow band of weft-faced plain weave, red (bottom)
NOTE: pile upside down in relation to object orientation, indicating that the bag was woven as one of a pair, with the pile of the second bag in the normal direction
1997.142.9

3. Salor bag *(chuval)*

31 × 53 in. (79 × 135 cm)
WARP: wool, ivory, Z2S; alternate warps slightly depressed
WEFT: wool, pink, 2Z; 2 shots
PILE: wool, 2Z; silk, Z2S
knot: asymmetrical, predominately open on the right, some open on left
count: 15 × 20–21 per in. = 300–315 per sq. in.

colors: rust red, red, magenta (silk only), dark blue, medium blue, ivory, greenish brown (7)

SELVAGES: no original selvages

ENDS: no original end finishes

1997.142.8

4. Salor trapping

36 × 85 in. (91 × 216 cm)

WARP: wool, light gray brown, Z2S; alternate warps slightly depressed

WEFT: wool, ivory, Z2S; 2 shots

PILE: wool, 2Z; silk, Z3S

knot: asymmetrical, open on the left

count: 14 horiz. × 17 vert. per in. = 238 per sq. in.

colors: rust red, brick red, carmine red (silk), white, medium blue, dark green, brown, dark yellow (8)

SELVAGES: no original selvages

ENDS: no original end finishes

NOTE: pile upside down in relation to object orientation

1997.142.7

5. Saryk main carpet

113 × 93 in. (287 × 236 cm)

WARP: wool, light gray brown, Z2S; alternate warps slightly depressed

WEFT: wool, light gray brown, Z2S; 2 shots

PILE: wool, 2Z

knot: symmetrical

count: 9 horiz. × 13–14 vert. per in. = 117–126 per sq. in.

colors: brick red, medium blue, blue green, ivory, apricot, brown (6)

SELVAGES: 3-rib reinforced selvage (2 warp ends per rib); brown wool reinforcement

ENDS: red weft-faced plain weave with single blue stripe (top and bottom)

1997.142.3

6. Saryk main carpet

91 × 88 in. (231 × 223 cm)

WARP: wool, medium brown to light gray brown, Z2S; alternate warps slightly depressed

WEFT: wool, light brown, 2Z; 2 shots

PILE: wool, 2Z; cotton, 2Z

knot: symmetrical

count: 9–10 horiz. × 14–15 vert. per in. = 126–150 per sq. in.

colors: red brown, dull apricot, dark blue, brown black, ivory, white (cotton only) (6)

SELVAGES: 12 warps, reinforced in pairs with brown wool, except for the outermost pair, which is overcast with red wool (one small section of original overcastting remains)

ENDS: no original end finishes

1997.142.1

7. Saryk door rug *(ensi)*

68 × 52 in. (173 × 132 cm)

WARP: wool, ivory, Z2S; alternate warps slightly depressed

WEFT: wool, ivory, Z2S; 2 shots

PILE: wool, 2Z

knot: symmetrical

count: 8 horiz. × 12 vert. per in. = 96 per sq. in.

colors: pale brick red, dark blue, medium blue, dark brown, ivory, pale yellow (6)

SELVAGES: no original selvages

ENDS: no original end finishes

1997.142.2

8. Saryk bag *(torba)*

17 × 44 in. (43 × 112 cm)

WARP: wool, ivory, Z2S; alternate warps slightly depressed

WEFT: wool, light brown, 2Z

PILE: wool, 2Z; cotton, Z2S

knot: symmetrical, slightly depressed

count: 12 horiz. × 18 vert. per in. = 216 per sq. in.

colors: brick red, dark blue, dark apricot, dark brown, medium brown (lighter at tips) ivory, white (cotton only) (7)

SELVAGES: no original selvages

ENDS: weft-faced plain weave with ivory band, hemmed (top); not original (bottom)

1997.142.4

9. Saryk(?) tent band *(ak yüp)* (fragment)

Warp-predominant plain weave with symmetrical knotting on alternate warps

48 × 14 in. (122 × 36 cm)

WARP: wool, ivory, Z2S

WEFT: wool, ivory, 2Z

PILE: wool, 2Z

knot: symmetrical; on alternate warps

count: 16–17 horiz. × 12 vert. per in. = 192–204 per sq. in.

colors: medium red brown, dark blue, medium red (3)

SELVAGES: 4 warps, overcast with dark brown wool

ENDS: no original end finishes

1997.142.5

10. Tekke main carpet

105 × 88 in. (267 × 223 cm)

WARP: Tekke main carpet

WEFT: wool, brown, Z2S

PILE: wool, 2Z

knot: asymmetrical, open on the right

count: 10 horiz. × 12–13 vert. per in. = 120–130 per sq. in.

colors: brick red, rust red, dark blue, light blue, blue green, dark brown, ivory (7)

SELVAGES: no original selvages

ENDS: no original end finishes

1997.142.11

11. Tekke main carpet

105 × 88 in. (267 × 223 cm)

WARP: wool, ivory, Z2S

WEFT: wool, 2Z; 2 shots

PILE: wool, 2Z

knot: asymmetrical, open on the right

count: 10 horiz. × 9–10 vert. per in. = 90–100 per sq. in.

colors: pale brick red, ivory, yellow brown, light blue, dark blue, apricot (6)
SELVAGES: no original selvages
ENDS: no original end finishes
1997.142.13

yellow, brown, ivory, apricot, blue green (8)
SELVAGES: no original selvages
ENDS: not original
1997.142.14

colors: brick red, medium blue, blue green, ivory, apricot, brown (6)
SELVAGES: no original selvages
ENDS: no original end finishes
1997.195.32

12. Tekke main carpet

95 × 81 in. (241 × 206 cm)
WARP: wool, ivory, Z2S
WEFT: wool, gray brown, Z2S, 2 shots
PILE: wool, Z2
knot: asymmetrical, open on the right
count: 13 horiz. × 13 vert. per in. = 169 per sq. in.
colors: dark red brown, brown, yellow, apricot, light blue, dark blue, ivory (7)
SELVAGES: 2-rib reinforced selvage; blue wool (Z2S) reinforcement
ENDS: no original end finishes
1997.195.30

13. Tekke main carpet

94 × 87 in. (239 × 221 cm)
WARP: wool, ivory, Z2S
WEFT: wool, ivory, Z2S; 2 shots
PILE: wool, Z2
knot: asymmetrical, open on the right
count: 10–11 horiz. × 16 vert. per in. = 160–176 per sq. in.
colors: brick red, dark blue, light blue, blue green, brown, dark rust red, ivory (7)
SELVAGES: no original selvages
ENDS: band of red weft-faced plain weave with a narrow blue stripe at each side (top and bottom)
1997.142.12

14. Tekke rug (fragment)

41 × 46 in. (104 × 117 cm)
WARP: wool, ivory, Z2S
WEFT: wool, brown, Z2S; 2 shots
PILE: wool, 2Z
knot: asymmetrical, open on the right
count: 10 horiz. × 11 vert. per in. = 110 per sq. in.
colors: brick red, light blue, dark blue,

15. Tekke rug

48 × 33 in. (122 × 84 cm)
WARP: wool, light brown, Z2S
WEFT: wool, light brown, Z2S; 2 shots
PILE: wool, 2Z
knot: asymmetrical, open on the right
count: 11–12 horiz. × 16–18 vert. per in. = 187–216 per sq. in.
colors: brick red, blue, blue green, brown, apricot, ivory (6)
SELVAGES: no original selvages
ENDS: no original end finishes
1997.142.15

16. Tekke rug (fragment)

47 × 30 in. (119 × 76 cm)
WARP: wool, ivory to light brown, Z2S; alternate warps slightly depressed
WEFT: wool, ivory to light brown, Z2S; 2 shots
PILE: wool, 2-ply
knot: asymmetrical, open on the right
count: 12 horiz. × 18 vert. per in. = 216 per sq. in.
colors: brick red, blue, blue green, ivory, brown, apricot (6)
SELVAGES: no original selvages
ENDS: no original end (top); wide band of red with 3 groups of 3 dark blue stripes and a row of motifs in knotted pile on inner section of band
1997.142.16

17. Tekke door rug (ensi)

63 × 46 in. (160 × 117 cm)
WARP: wool, ivory, Z2S
WEFT: wool, ivory, Z2S; 2 shots
PILE: wool, 2Z
knot: asymmetrical, open on the right
count: 8 horiz. × 12 vert. per in. = 96 per sq. in.

colors: brick red, medium blue, blue green, ivory, apricot, brown (6)
SELVAGES: no original selvages
ENDS: no original end finishes
1997.195.32

18. Tekke door rug (ensi)

56 × 40 in. (142 × 102 cm)
WARP: wool, light brown, Z2S
WEFT: wool, light brown, Z2S; 2 shots
PILE: wool, 2Z
knot: asymmetrical, open on the right
count: 10 horiz. × 17 vert. per in. = 170 per sq. in.
colors: dark brick red, dark blue, medium blue, bright red, medium brown, ivory (6)
SELVAGES: no original selvages
ENDS: no original end finishes
1997.142.19

19. Tekke bag (chuval)

34 × 52 in. (86 × 132 cm)
WARP: wool, light brown, Z2S
WEFT: wool, Z2S; 2 shots
PILE: wool, 2Z; silk, Z2S
knot: asymmetrical, open on the right
count: 11 horiz. × 14 vert. per in. = 154 per sq. in.
colors: red brown, dark blue, medium blue, carmine red, magenta (silk only), ivory, dark brown (7)
SELVAGES: no original selvages
ENDS: no original end finishes
1997.142.10

20. Tekke bag (chuval)

19 × 43 in. (48 × 109 cm)
WARP: wool, light brown, Z2S
WEFT: wool, light brown, Z2S; 2 shots
PILE: wool, 2Z
knot: asymmetrical, open on the right
count: 12 horiz. × 22–23 vert. per in. = 264–276 per sq. in.
colors: brick red, blue, blue green, ivory, brown, apricot (6)
SELVAGES: no original selvages

ENDS: band of ivory weft-faced plain weave, hemmed (top); not original (bottom)

1997.195.35

21. Tekke bag (ak chuval)

34 × 44 in. (86 × 112 cm)
WARP: wool, ivory, Z2S
WEFT: wool, dark brown; predominately 1 shot in narrow pile bands, 2 shots in pile alem
PILE: wool, 2Z; cotton, Z2S
knot: asymmetrical, open on the right
count: 2 horiz. × 22 vert. per in. = 264 per sq. in.
colors: dark red brown, carmine red, dark brown, dark blue, white (cotton only) (5)
SELVAGES: 4 warps interlaced in pairs by foundation weft
ENDS: no original end finishes

1997.195.33

22. Tekke rug or bag

45 × 39 in. (114 × 99 cm)
WARP: wool, ivory, Z2S
WEFT: wool, ivory, Z2S; 2 shots
PILE: wool, 2Z
knot: asymmetrical, open on the right
count: 10 horiz. × 15 vert. per in. = 150 per sq. in.
colors: brick red, rust red, brown, ivory, blue, blue green (6)
SELVAGES: no original selvages
ENDS: no original end finishes

1997.195.31

23. Tekke bag (torba)

18 × 41 in. (46 × 104 cm)
WARP: wool, light brown, Z2S
WEFT: wool, medium brown, Z2S; 2 shots
PILE: wool, 2Z
knot: asymmetrical, open on the right
count: 11 horiz. × 16 vert. per in. = 176 per sq. in.
colors: dark brick red, dark blue, light blue, dark brown, ivory, apricot (6)

SELVAGES: no original selvages
ENDS: no original end finishes

1997.142.20

24. Tekke door surround (kapunuk)

37 × 43 in. (94 × 109 cm)
WARP: wool, ivory, Z2S
WEFT: wool, ivory, Z2S; 2 shots
knot: asymmetrical, open on the right
count: 12 horiz. × 19–20 vert. per in. = 228–240 per sq. in.
colors: brick red, apricot, blue, dark brown, ivory (5)
SELVAGES: overcast with dark blue wool, Z2S (possibly not original)
ENDS: ivory weft-faced plain weave, hemmed (top and bottom), with polychrome knotted fringe at bottom
NOTE: pile upside down in relation to object orientation

1997.195.1

25. Tekke door surround (kapunuk)

35 × 46 in. (90 × 117 cm)
WARP: wool, ivory, Z2S
WEFT: wool, ivory, Z2S; 2 shots
PILE: wool, 2Z
knot: asymmetrical, open on the right
count: 11 horiz. × 18–19 vert. per in. = 198–209 per sq. in.
colors: ivory, dark green, brick red, apricot, dark blue, pale yellow, purple brown, dark brown (8)
SELVAGES: overcast with blue wool, Z2S (probably not original)
ENDS: ivory plain weave band, hemmed (top); polychrome knotted fringe (bottom right)

1997.142.18

26. Tekke wedding trapping (asmalyk)

35 × 51 in. (89 × 130 cm)
WARP: wool, ivory, Z2S
WEFT: wool, medium brown, Z2S; 2 shots
PILE: wool, 2Z
knot: asymmetrical, open on the right
count: 12 horiz. × 20 vert. per in. = 240 per sq. in.
colors: brick red, red orange, dark blue, ivory, undyed brown (5)
SELVAGES: no original selvages
ENDS: no original end finishes

1997.195.34

27. Rug made from five pieces of Tekke tent band lengths

Warp-faced plain weave with symmetrical knotting on alternate warps
78 × 58 in. (198 × 147 cm), as sewn
WARP: wool, ivory, Z2S
WEFT: wool, ivory, Z2S
PILE: wool, 2Z
knot: symmetrical, on alternate warps
count: 18 horiz. × 28 vert. per in. = 504 per sq. in.
colors: ivory, rust red, dark blue, light brown (4)
SELVAGES: no original selvages
ENDS: no original end finishes

1997.142.17

28. Eagle gul main carpet, group II

96 × 74 in. (244 × 188 cm)
WARP: wool, ivory, Z2S
WEFT: 1 wool yarn (ivory, Z2S) and 1 cotton yarn (Z2S); 2 shots (1 shot wool alternating with 1 shot cotton)
PILE: wool, Z2S
knot: asymmetrical, open on the right
count: 9.5 × 10 horiz. × 17–18 vert. per in. = 162–180 per sq. in.
colors: red brown, ivory, rust, dark blue, medium blue, blue green, dark brown (7)
SELVAGES: no original selvages

ENDS: brick red weft-faced plain weave with several figures in knotted pile (top and bottom)
1997.195.43

29. Eagle *gul* main carpet, group III

88 × 63 in. (224 × 160 cm)
WARP: wool, ivory, Z2S
WEFT: wool, Z2S; 2 shots
PILE: wool, 2Z and 3Z
knot: symmetrical, open on the left
count: 11 horiz. × 14 vert. per in. = 154 per sq. in.
colors: red brown, dark blue, light blue, pale rust, ivory, brown (6)
SELVAGES: no original selvages
ENDS: no original end finishes
1997.195.39

30. Eagle *gul* bag *(chuval),* group II

34 × 43 in. (86 × 109 cm)
WARP: wool, light and dark brown, Z2S
WEFT: wool, reddish brown, Z2S, 2 shots
PILE: wool, 2Z
knot: asymmetrical, open on the right
count: 10 horiz. × 13–14 vert. per in. = 130–140 per sq. in.
colors: brown, blue, blue green, ivory, dark brown, apricot (6)
SELVAGES: no original selvages
ENDS: no original end finishes
1997.142.30

31. Yomut main carpet

99 × 68 in. (252 × 173 cm)
WARP: wool, ivory, Z2S
WEFT: wool, 2Z; 2 shots
PILE: wool, 2Z
knot: symmetrical
count: 9 horiz. × 13 vert. per in. = 117 per sq. in.
colors: dark brick red, dark blue, light blue, blue green, pale yellow, rust red, dark brown, ivory (8)

SELVAGES: no original selvages
ENDS: no original end finishes
1997.195.40

32. Yomut main carpet, reconstructed from fragments

114 × 69 in. (290 × 175 cm)
WARP: wool, light brown, Z2S
WEFT: wool, light brown, Z2S; 2 shots
PILE: wool, 2Z
knot: symmetrical
count: 9 horiz. × 12 vert. per in. = 108 per sq. in.
colors: dark red brown, ivory, pale rust red, pale yellow, medium blue, brown black (7)
SELVAGES: no original selvages
ENDS: no original end finishes
1997.195.37

33. Yomut main carpet

114 × 64 in. (290 × 163 cm)
WARP: wool, light brown, Z2S
WEFT: wool, brown, Z2S; 2 shots
PILE: wool, 2Z
knot: symmetrical
count: 10 horiz. × 9 vert. per in. = 90 per sq. in.
colors: purple brown, apricot, medium blue, blue green, pale yellow, ivory, dark brown (7)
SELVAGES: no original selvages
ENDS: traces of ivory plain weave
1997.142.21

34. Yomut main carpet

119 × 68 in. (302 × 173 cm)
WARP: wool, light brown, Z2S
WEFT: wool, light brown, Z2S; 2 shots
PILE: wool, 2Z
knot: symmetrical
count: 9–10 horiz. × 11 vert. per in. = 99–110 per sq. in.
colors: red brown, pale apricot, red, dark blue, light blue, ivory, brown (7)
SELVAGES: no original selvages
ENDS: brown, weft-faced plain weave

(top); band of brown weft-faced plain weave terminating in 2 bands of ivory separated by 2 rows of blue and red knotted pile (bottom)
1997.142.23

35. Yomut main carpet

113 × 62 in. (287 × 158 cm)
WARP: wool, light brown, Z2S
WEFT: wool, light brown, Z2S; 2 shots
PILE: wool, 2Z
knot: symmetrical
count: 8 horiz. × 12 vert. per in. = 96 per sq. in.
colors: red brown, rust red, dark blue, blue green, yellow, ivory, dark brown (7)
SELVAGES: no original selvages
ENDS: no original end finishes
1997.142.22

36. Yomut main carpet

96 × 60 in. (244 × 152 cm)
WARP: wool, light brown, Z2S
WEFT: wool, light brown, Z2S; 2 shots
PILE: wool, 2Z
knot: symmetrical
count: 8 horiz. × 14 vert. per in. = 112 per sq. in.
colors: red brown, rust red, dark blue, light blue, yellow, ivory, dark brown (7)
SELVAGES: no original selvages
ENDS: no original end finishes
1997.142.24

37. Yomut main carpet

118 × 64 in. (300 × 163 cm)
WARP: wool, light brown, Z2S
WEFT: wool, light brown, Z2S; 2 shots
PILE: wool, 2Z
knot: symmetrical
count: 10 horiz. × 14 vert. per in. = 140 per sq. in.
colors: dark red brown, pale rust red, dark blue, ivory, brown black (5)
SELVAGES: no original selvages
ENDS: no original end finishes
1997.195.38

38. Yomut main carpet

96 × 61 in. (244 × 155 cm)

WARP: wool, ivory, Z2S

WEFT: wool, ivory, Z2S; 2 shots

PILE: wool, 2Z

knot: symmetrical

count: 9 horiz. × 12 vert. per in. = 108 per sq. in.

colors: red brown, blue, blue green, apricot, ivory, dark brown, yellow (7)

SELVAGES: no original selvages

ENDS: no original end finishes

1997.195.36

39. Yomut door rug *(ensi)*

58 × 48 in. (147 × 123 cm)

WARP: wool, ivory to brown, Z2S

WEFT: wool, ivory to brown, Z2S; 2 shots

PILE: wool, 2Z

knot: symmetrical

count: 9 horiz. × 14 vert. per in. = 126 per sq. in.

colors: red brown, peach, dark blue, light blue, blue green, ivory, dark brown, dull yellow (8)

SELVAGES: no original selvages

ENDS: no original end finishes

1997.142.27

40. Yomut bag *(chuval)*

31 × 46 in. (79 × 117 cm)

WARP: wool, light brown, Z2S

WEFT: wool (light brown, Z2S) and cotton (white, Z2S); 2 shots (1 shot cotton alternating with 1 shot wool) in most of rug

PILE: wool, 2Z

knot: symmetrical

count: 9 horiz. × 18–19 vert. per in. = 162–171 per sq. in.

colors: red brown, pale red, blue, blue green, ivory, dark brown, pale yellow (7)

SELVAGES: no original selvages

ENDS: weft-faced plain weave, hemmed (top); not original (bottom)

1997.195.2

41. Yomut bag *(chuval)*

33 × 48 in. (84 × 122 cm)

WARP: wool, gray brown, Z2S

WEFT: wool, gray brown, Z2S; 2 shots

PILE: wool, 2Z

knot: symmetrical

count: 7 horiz. × 13–14 vert. per in. = 91–98 per sq. in.

colors: purple brown, dark blue, light blue, ivory, pale rust, yellow, dark brown (7)

SELVAGES: no original selvages

ENDS: no original end finishes

1997.195.5

42. Yomut bag *(chuval)*

Weft-faced plain weave with discontinuous supplementary-weft wrapping

31 × 47 in. (79 × 119 cm)

WARP: wool, brown, Z2S

WEFTS: Foundation: wool, brick red, Z2S

Supplementary: wool, Z2S and cotton Z2S (machine spun?); dark apricot, dark blue, ivory (cotton only), blue green (5)

SELVAGES: no original selvages

ENDS: red weft-faced plain weave with 2 narrow bands of weft substitution at edge and band of brown weft-faced plain weave, turned under and hemmed (top); not original (bottom)

1997.142.29

43. Yomut bag *(kap)*

18 × 37 in. (46 × 94 cm)

WARP: wool, light brown, Z2S

WEFT: wool, light brown, Z2S; 2 shots

PILE: wool, 2Z

knot: symmetrical

count: 11 horiz. × 18–19 vert. per in. = 198–209 per sq. in.

colors: dark brick red, blue green, dark blue, dark brown, dark ivory (5)

SELVAGES: no original selvages

ENDS: no original end finishes

NOTE: pile upside down in relation to object orientation

1997.142.28

44. Yomut wedding trapping *(asmalyk)*

29 × 48 in. (74 × 122 cm)

WARP: wool, ivory, Z2S

WEFT: wool, light apricot, Z2S; 2 shots

PILE: wool, 2Z

knot: symmetrical

count: 9 horiz. × 12 vert. per in. = 108 per sq. in.

colors: light brick red, red brown, dark brown, ivory, yellow, dark blue, medium blue (7)

SELVAGES: not visible

ENDS: narrow bands of red weft-faced plain weave, hemmed (top and bottom)

EDGING: applied medium-red wool braid around entire perimeter of trapping

1997.195.4

45. Yomut wedding trapping *(asmalyk)*

26 × 41 in. (66 × 104 cm)

WARP: wool, brown, Z2S

WEFT: wool, brown, Z2S; 2 shots

PILE: wool, 2Z

knot: symmetrical

count: 9 horiz. × 10 vert. per in. = 90 per sq. in.

colors: brick red, dark blue, light blue, blue green, ivory, apricot, dark brown, light red brown (8)

SELVAGES: no original selvages

ENDS: 2-color (red and blue) chaining at upper edge of knotting, followed by 1 brown and 1 blue stripe, terminating in brick red weft-faced plain weave (top); 2-color (red and blue) chaining and a band of brick red weft-faced plain weave (bottom)

1997.195.41

46. Yomut wedding trapping *(asmalyk)*

50 × 31 in. (127 × 79 cm)

WARP: wool, ivory, 2 strands

WEFT: wool, ivory, Z2S; 2 shots

PILE: wool, 2Z

knot: asymmetrical, open on the left
count: 8 horiz. × 20 vert. per in. = 160 per sq. in.
colors: rust red, dark blue, medium blue, brown black, peach, ivory (6)
SELVAGES: 2-rib reinforced selvage; peach and medium blue wool reinforcement
ENDS: brown weft-faced plain weave, hemmed (top); brown weft-faced plain weave (bottom)
1997.142.31

47. Yomut tent-pole cover (ok bash), unsewn

27 × 24 in. (69 × 61 cm)
WARP: wool, light brown, Z2S
WEFT: wool, light brown, Z2S; 2 shots
PILE: wool, Z2S
knot: symmetrical
count: 9 horiz. × 14–15 vert. per in. = 126–135 per sq. in.
colors: brick red, blue, dull yellow, brown, blue green, buff pink (faded) (6)
SELVAGE: overcast with blue and red wool, Z2S (probably not original)
ENDS: no original end finishes
NOTE: An *ok bash* is woven perpendicular to the plane of view so that the pile lies sideways, one of the selvages becomes the upper edge of the cover, and the ends of the weaving are joined to become the side seam of the cover.
1997.195.42

48. Yomut tent-pole cover (ok bash)

40 × 23 in. (102 × 58 cm), height × circumference
WARP: wool, ivory, Z2S
WEFT: wool, ivory, Z2S
PILE: wool, Z2
knot: symmetrical
count: 9 horiz. per in. × 16 vert. per in. = 144 per sq. in.
colors: brick red, red brown, apricot, dark brown, ivory (5)

SELVAGE: 4 warp units, reinforced in pairs by blue wool (Z2S)
ENDS: band of ivory weft-faced plain weave, hemmed, and overcast with red and blue wool
NOTE: See note, plate 47.
1997.195.3

49. Chodor main carpet

86 × 78 in. (218 × 198 cm)
WARP: wool, gray brown, Z2S
WEFT: wool (gray brown, Z2S) and cotton (white, Z2S); 2 shots (in some areas wool only, in some cotton only, and in others the wool and cotton are used in alternating shots)
PILE: wool, 2Z
knot: asymmetrical, open on the right
count: 8 horiz. × 12 vert. per in. = 96 per sq. in.
colors: dark purple, dark salmon, ivory, light brown, blue green, gray green (6)
SELVAGES: no original selvages
ENDS: no original end finishes
1997.142.32

50. Chodor main carpet

122 × 82 in. (310 × 208 cm)
WARP: wool or goat hair, gray brown, Z2S
WEFT: wool or goat hair (gray brown, Z2S) and cotton (white, Z2S); 2 shots (both yarns used together in each shot)
PILE: wool, 2Z and 3Z (blue, green brown, salmon)
knot: asymmetrical, open on the right
count: 7 horiz. × 10–11 vert. per in. = 70–77 per sq. in.
colors: greenish brown, salmon, dark blue, pale yellow, ivory, dark brown (6)
SELVAGES: 6-rib (left) and 7-rib (right) reinforced selvage; dark brown wool or goat hair reinforcement
ENDS: brown weft-faced plain weave (top)
1997.142.33

51. Chodor prayer rug (namazlyk)

60 × 37 in. (152 × 94 cm)
WARP: wool or goat hair, brown, Z2S
WEFT: wool (brown) and cotton (white); 2 shots (1 shot of wool and 1 shot of cotton in alternation for $^1/_3$ of rug, only cotton wefts in the remainder)
PILE: wool, Z2S
knot: asymmetrical, open on the right
count: 7 horiz. × 14 vert. per in. = 98 per sq. in.
colors: pale red, purple brown, dark blue, ivory, pale yellow (5)
SELVAGES: 4-rib reinforced selvage (2 warps per rib); brown goat hair reinforcement
ENDS: no original end finishes
1997.142.34

52. Chodor bag (chuval)

29 × 43 in. (74 × 109 cm)
WARP: wool, light gray brown, Z2S
WEFT: wool, light gray brown, Z2S; 2 shots
PILE: wool, 2Z
knot: asymmetrical, open on the right
count: 9 horiz. × 17–18 vert. per in. = 153–162 per sq. in.
colors: purple brown, ivory, brick red, blue, blue green, dull yellow, dark brown (7)
SELVAGES: no original selvages
ENDS: brown and ivory striped weft-faced plain weave band, hemmed (top); not original (bottom)
1997.142.35

53. Arabachi main carpet

126 × 82 in. (320 × 208 cm)
WARP: wool or goat hair, dark gray brown, Z2S; alternate warps slightly depressed
WEFT: wool or goat hair (dark gray brown, Z2S) and cotton (white, Z2S); 2 shots (1 shot wool alternating with 1 shot cotton)

PILE: wool, 2Z

knot: asymmetrical, open on the left

count: 8 horiz. × 11 vert. per in. = 88 per sq. in.

colors: red brown, persimmon red, light blue, dark blue, brown, yellow, ivory (7)

SELVAGES: 2-rib reinforced selvage; light blue and red brown wool alternating to form checks

ENDS: long ends of red brown weft-predominant plain weave, with 4 groups of 3 dark blue or light blue stripes (top and bottom)

1997.195.23

54. Arabachi door rug (ensi)

102 × 82 in. (259 × 208 cm)

WARP: wool, gray brown to red brown, Z2S

WEFT: wool (gray brown) and cotton (white); 2 shots (1 shot wool alternating with 1 shot cotton)

PILE: wool, 2Z

knot: asymmetrical, open on the right

count: 10 horiz. × 10 vert. per in. = 100 per sq. in.

colors: purplish brown, rust red, carmine red, dark blue, medium blue, brown, ivory (7)

SELVAGES: no original selvages

ENDS: no original end finishes

1997.195.24

55. Ersari main carpet

93 × 50 in. (236 × 127 cm)

WARP: wool, dark gray brown, Z2S

WEFT: wool, brown, Z2S; 2 shots

PILE: wool, Z2S

knot: asymmetrical, open on the right

count: 6 horiz. × 7 vert. per in. = 42 per sq. in.

colors: brick red, dark brown, yellow, apricot, blue, ivory (6)

SELVAGES: 6-rib reinforced selvage (3 warps per rib); brown goat hair reinforcement

ENDS: no original end finishes

1997.142.37

56. Ersari main carpet

102 × 82 in. (259 × 208 cm)

WARP: wool, gray brown; Z2S

WEFT: wool, gray brown, Z2S; 2 shots

PILE: wool, Z2S

knot: asymmetrical, open on the right

count: 7 horiz. × 7 vert. per in. = 49 per sq. in.

colors: light brick red, apricot, bright yellow, dark blue, light blue, dark brown, white (7)

SELVAGES: 3-rib reinforced selvage (3 warps per rib); brown goat hair reinforcement

ENDS: brick red weft-faced plain weave with 1 dark blue stripe (top); same as top but with 2 dark blue stripes (bottom)

1997.195.25

57. Ersari main carpet

112 × 87 in. (284 × 221 cm)

WARP: wool, medium gray brown, Z2S

WEFT: wool, medium gray brown, Z2S

PILE: wool, Z2S

knot: asymmetrical, open on the right

count: 9 horiz. × 10–11 vert. per in. = 90–99 per sq. in.

colors: dark brick red, ivory, apricot, pale yellow, dark blue, light blue, blue green, brown black (8)

SELVAGES: No original selvages

ENDS: no original end finishes

1997.195.7

58. Ersari main carpet

112 × 84 in. (284 × 213 cm)

WARP: wool, light brown to gray brown, Z2S

WEFT: wool, gray brown, Z2S; 2 shots

PILE: wool, 2Z

knot: asymmetrical, open on the right

count: 8–9 horiz. × 9 vert. per in. = 72–81 per sq. in.

colors: brick red, dark blue, medium blue, blue green, brown, ivory, bright yellow (7)

SELVAGES: 3-rib reinforced selvage

(3 warps per rib), brown goat hair reinforcing

ENDS: no original end finishes

1997.195.27

59. Ersari main carpet (fragment)

60 × 24 in. (152 × 61 cm)

WARP: wool, light gray brown, Z2S

WEFT: wool, light gray brown, Z2S; 2 shots

PILE: wool, Z2S

knot: asymmetrical, open on the left

count: 7 horiz. × 10 vert. per in. = 70 per sq. in.

colors: brick red, apricot, blue, pale yellow, light blue, ivory, dark brown (7)

SELVAGES: no original selvages

ENDS: no original end finishes

1997.195.28

60. Ersari or Chub Bash main carpet

108 × 81 in. (274 × 206 cm)

WARP: wool, gray brown, Z2S

WEFT: wool, gray brown, Z2S; 2 shots

PILE: wool, 2Z

knot: asymmetrical, open on the right

count: 7.5 horiz. × 8 vert. per in. = 60 per sq. in.

colors: purple brown, light blue, medium blue, ivory, yellow, green, apricot (with pronounced abrash), dark brown (8)

SELVAGES: no original selvages

ENDS: no original end finishes

1997.195.22

61. Ersari bag (chuval)

41 × 60 in. (104 × 152 cm)

WARP: wool, gray brown, Z2S

WEFT: wool, gray brown, Z2S; 2 shots

PILE: wool, Z2S

knot: asymmetrical, open on the right

count: 6½–7 horiz. × 12 vert. per in. = 78–84 per sq. in.

colors: brick red, dark blue, light blue, apricot, blue green, dark brown, yellow, ivory (8)

Turkman *yurt* interior, near Ashkabad, early twentieth century. Coverlets used for bedding are stacked on top of a wooden box covered with a pile carpet. In the foreground are a hot water vessel, teapot, samovar, winding wheel, and skeins of wool.

SELVAGES: no original selvages
ENDS: no original end finishes
NOTE: pile upside down in relation to object orientation
1997.195.17

62. Ersari door rug *(ensi)*

67 × 48 in. (170 × 123 cm)
WARP: wool, gray brown, Z2S
WEFT: wool, gray brown, Z2S; 2 shots
PILE: wool, 2Z
knot: asymmetrical, open on the right
count: 8 horiz. × 11 vert. per in. = 88 per sq. in.
colors: brick red, blue, blue green, pale yellow, ivory, dark brown, apricot (7)
SELVAGES: no original selvages

ENDS: ivory and rust weft-faced plain weave band, hemmed (top); not original (bottom)
1997.195.29

63. Ersari bag *(chuval)*

37 × 63 in. (94 × 160 cm)
WARP: wool, gray brown, Z2S
WEFT: wool, gray brown, Z2S; 2 shots
PILE: wool, Z2S
knot: asymmetrical, open on the right
count: 7 horiz. × 11 vert. per in. = 77 per sq. in.
colors: brick red, dark blue, light blue, ivory, yellow, blue green, apricot (7)
SELVAGES: no original selvages
ENDS: red plain weave (fragmentary)
1997.195.10

64. Ersari bag *(chuval)*

36 × 65 in. (91 × 165 cm)
WARP: wool, gray brown, Z2S
WEFT: wool, gray brown, Z2S; 2 shots
PILE: wool, Z2S
knot: asymmetrical, open on the right
count: 8 horiz. × 10 vert. per in. = 80 per sq. in.
colors: brick red, ivory, dark brown, green (with pronounced abrash), blue (5)
SELVAGES: no original selvages
ENDS: no original end finishes
1997.195.18

65. Ersari bag (torba)

15 × 62 in. (38 × 158 cm)
WARP: wool, gray brown, Z2S
WEFT: wool, brown, Z2S; 2 shots
PILE: wool, Z2S
knot: asymmetrical, open on the left
count: 9 horiz. × 11 vert. per in. = 99 per sq. in.
colors: brick red, apricot, green, dark blue, light blue, brown, ivory (7)
SELVAGES: no original selvages
ENDS: no original end finishes
1997.195.19

66. Ersari carpet (fragment)

98 × 75 in. (249 × 191 cm)
WARP: wool, gray brown, Z2S
WEFT: wool, gray brown, Z2S; 2 shots
PILE: wool, Z2S
knot: asymmetrical, open on the right
count: 10 horiz. × 11 vert. per in. = 110 per sq. in.
colors: brick red, light blue, dark blue, blue green, pale yellow, ivory, apricot (7)
SELVAGES: no original selvages
ENDS: no original end finishes
1997.195.26a

67. Ersari carpet (fragment)

89 × 44 in. (226 × 112 cm)
WARP: wool or goat hair, light brown, Z2S
WEFT: wool or goat hair, light brown, Z2S; 2 shots
PILE: wool, 2Z
knot: asymmetrical, open on the left
count: 8 horiz. × 8 vert. per in. = 64 per sq. in.
colors: red, yellow, ivory, green, apricot, medium brown (6)
SELVAGES: 2-rib reinforced selvage (3 warps per rib)
ENDS: no original end finishes
1997.195.26b

68. Kizil Ayak main carpet

97 × 81 in. (246 × 206 cm)
WARP: wool, ivory, Z2S
WEFT: wool, ivory, Z2S; 2 shots
PILE: wool, 2Z
knot: asymmetrical, open on the right
count: 8–9 horiz. × 12–13 vert. per in. = 96–117 per sq. in.
colors: brick red, rust red, blue, dark green, yellow, ivory, dark brown (7)
SELVAGES: no original selvages
ENDS: no original end finishes
1997.195.16

69. Kizil Ayak or Ersari bag (chuval)

38 × 58 in. (97 × 147 cm)
WARP: wool, light brown, Z2S
WEFT: wool, light brown; Z2S; 2 shots
PILE: wool, 2Z; silk, Z2S
knot: asymmetrical, open on the right
count: 8½ horiz. × 17 vert. per in. = 144 per sq. in.
colors: brick red, medium brown, blue, green, bright yellow, apricot, ivory, magenta (silk only) (8)
SELVAGES: no original selvages
ENDS: no original end finishes
1997.195.14

70. Beshir carpet

95 × 51 in. (241 × 130 cm)
WARP: wool, dark gray brown, Z2S
WEFT: wool, light to medium gray brown, 2Z; 2 shots
PILE: wool, 2Z
knot: asymmetrical, open on right
count: 6–7 horiz. × 9–11 vert. per in. = 56–77 per sq. in.
colors: red, dark blue, medium blue, blue green (with pronounced abrash), yellow, dark brown, ivory (7)
SELVAGES: 6 warps reinforced in pairs by medium blue wool (4Z)
ENDS: red weft-faced plain weave (top and bottom)
1997.195.36

71. Beshir carpet

153 × 80 in. (389 × 203 cm)
WARP: wool, gray brown, Z2S
WEFT: wool, gray brown with occasional reddish tinge, Z2S; 2 shots
PILE: wool, Z2S
knot: asymmetrical, open on the right
count: 7–7½ horiz. × 7 vert. per in. = 49–53 per sq. in.
colors: brick red, pale brick red, blue green, medium blue, dark blue, yellow, dark brown, ivory (8)
SELVAGES: 2-rib reinforced selvage; light red wool reinforcing
ENDS: no original end finishes
1997.195.8

72. Beshir carpet (fragment)

31 × 28 in. (79 × 71 cm)
WARP: wool, light brown, Z2S
WEFT: wool, light brown, Z2S; 2 shots
PILE: wool, Z2S
knot: asymmetrical, open on the right
count: 7–7½ horiz. × 8 vert. per in. = 56–59 per sq. in.
colors: brick red, yellow, apricot, blue green, blue, brown, ivory (7)
SELVAGES: no original selvages
ENDS: no original end finishes
1997.195.12

73. Beshir carpet

134 × 105 in. (340 × 267 cm)
WARP: wool, dark gray brown, Z2S
WEFT: wool, dark gray brown, Z2S; 2 shots
PILE: wool, Z2S
knot: asymmetrical, open on the right
count: 5½ horiz. × 6 vert. per in. = 33 per sq. in.
colors: brick red, medium blue, brown, yellow, ivory, apricot (6)
SELVAGES: no original selvages
ENDS: brick red weft-faced plain weave with 3 blue and 1 brown stripe (top) and 4 blue stripes (bottom)
1997.195.9

74. Beshir carpet

142 × 79 in. (361 × 201 cm)
WARP: wool, gray brown, Z2S
WEFT: wool, gray brown, Z2S; 2 shots
PILE: wool, Z2S
knot: asymmetrical, open on the right
count: 7 horiz. × 9 vert. per in. = 63 per sq. in.
colors: brick red (with pronounced abrash), light blue, dark blue, green, mustard yellow (with abrash), ivory, dark brown (7)
SELVAGES: no original selvages
ENDS: no original end finishes
1997.195.6

75. Beshir prayer rug *(namazlyk)*

70 × 45 in. (178 × 114 cm)
WARP: wool, gray brown, Z2S
WEFT: wool, gray brown, Z2S; 2 shots
PILE: wool, Z2S
knot: asymmetrical, open on the right
count: 8 horiz. × 9 vert. per in. = 72 per sq. in.
colors: brick red, green (with pronounced abrash), ivory, yellow, blue, dark brown (6)
SELVAGES: 2-rib reinforced selvage (3 warps per rib); brown goat hair reinforcing
ENDS: weft-faced plain weave with 3 blue stripes, terminating in a narrow band of ivory weft-faced plain weave (top and bottom)
1997.195.13

76. Beshir wedding trapping *(asmalyk)*

24 × 45 in. (61 × 114 cm)
WARP: wool, light brown, Z2S
WEFT: wool, light brown, Z2S; 2 shots
PILE: wool, 2Z
knot: asymmetrical, open on the right
count: 7 1/2 horiz. × 11 vert. per in. = 77–81 per sq. in.
colors: purple brown, ivory, dark blue, brown, apricot, blue green (6)

SELVAGES: no original selvages
ENDS: ivory weft-faced plain weave, hemmed
1997.195.15

77. Karakalpak or Uzbek carpet

87 × 54 in. (221 × 137 cm)
WARP: wool, brown, Z2S; alternate warps moderately depressed
WEFT: wool, brown, Z2S; 2 shots
PILE: wool, Z2S
knot: asymmetrical, open on the right
count: 8 horiz. × 7 vert. per in. = 56 per sq. in.
colors: pale rust red, brick red, dark blue, medium blue, dark yellow, ivory, dark brown (7)
SELVAGES: no original selvages
ENDS: no original end finishes
1997.195.21

78. Karakalpak or Uzbek carpet

116 × 61 in. (295 × 155 cm)
WARP: wool, ivory, Z2S
WEFT: wool, light brown, Z2S; 2 shots
PILE: wool, Z2S
knot: asymmetrical, open on the left
count: 7 horiz. × 7 1/2 vert. per in. = 53 per sq. in.
colors: purple brown, blue, light green, dull yellow, ivory, medium brown, dark blue gray with traces of red (8)
SELVAGES: no original selvages
ENDS: no original end finishes
1997.195.44

79. Tekke(?) rug *(palas)*

Plain weave with discontinuous supplementary-weft brocading; borders of discontinuous supplementary-weft brocading with 3/1 floats in vertical alignment (zili)
120 × 76 in. (305 × 193 cm)
WARP: wool, ivory, Z2S
WEFTS: Foundation: wool, brick red, 2Z
Supplementary: wool, Z2S; dark blue,

light blue, apricot, ivory, green, blue green
SELVAGES: 4 warps, reinforced in pairs
ENDS: weft-faced plain weave forming wide bands of red with groups of three blue stripes, terminating in a band of ivory plain weave (top and bottom)
1997.142.26

80. Tekke or Yomut rug *(palas)*

Plain weave with discontinuous supplementary-weft brocading
141 × 76 in. (358 × 193 cm)
WARP: wool, gray brown, Z2S
WEFTS: Foundation: wool, dull brick red, Z2
Supplementary: wool 2Z and Z2S; cotton, Z2S; brick red, light brick red, dark blue, blue green, white (cotton only)
SELVAGES: 6 warps, reinforced in pairs with blue wool (Z2S)
ENDS: wide bands of red plain weave with 4 sets of 3 narrow blue stripes, terminating in a narrow band of ivory weft-faced plain weave divided by a row of 2-color (blue and red) weft-twining
1997.142.25

81. Baluch prayer rug *(namazlyk)*

63 × 48 in. (160 × 122 cm)
WARP: wool, gray brown, Z2S
WEFT: wool, gray brown, Z2S; 2 shots
PILE: wool, Z2S
knot: asymmetrical, open on the left
count: 8 horiz. × 10 vert. per in. = 80 per sq. in.
colors: brick red, brown, blue, ivory, yellow (5)
SELVAGES: 8 warps, reinforced in pairs with brown wool or goat hair
ENDS: no original end finishes
1997.195.20

Glossary

We have not identified the languages of origin for any of the following terms because they are derived from a mixture of languages. Most of the terms for object types are Turkmen.

ABRASH. Horizontal variegation within a single color of the pile caused by the use of more than one dye lot or by uneven absorption of the dye.

AK CHUVAL. (*lit.*, white bag) Large bags distinguished by a broad end panel of white knotted pile decorated with treelike forms. The body of the bag face is decorated with alternating bands of weft-faced plain weave and knotted pile (pl. 21).

AK YÜP. (*lit.*, white band) A wide decorative band sometimes with all-over knotted pile but usually with pile confined to the pattern elements only (pls. 9, 27). The foundation is warp-faced plain weave, and as a result, adjacent warps are too closely spaced to accom-

modate the thickness of the pile yarn. The knots are "tied" only on the raised warps of an open shed, in effect around the first and third or second and fourth warps, i.e., around every other warp of the finished fabric.

ALEM, ELEM. A band or panel at the bottom of Turkmen bags, where it is usually knotted-pile, or at both ends of carpets and flatweaves, where it is almost always woven in weft-faced plain weave.

ASHIK. A diamond-shaped motif with a serrated outline; used primarily on borders and stripes.

ASMALYK. (*lit.,* hanging) Knotted-pile weavings, woven in pairs and usually pentagonal in shape, that decorated the flanks of the bride's camel in wedding processions. They were also sometimes displayed inside the tent on ceremonial or festive occasions (pls. 26, 44–46, 76).

Ashik

Chemche gul

Erre gul

AYNA GUL. (*lit.*, mirror gul) A term used for a chuval motif consisting of a rectangular compartment each enclosing a diamond-shaped element (fig. 14).

BOTEH. A cone-shaped motif that curves as it tapers toward its tip. It appears in carpet designs throughout the Middle East. The motif is often called "paisley" because of its appearance on woolen shawls woven in Paisley, Scotland, in the nineteenth century (pl. 72, outer border).

"C"-GUL. The term used in rug literature for a Yomut carpet motif, so named because of the C-shaped elements in its interior (fig. 6 and pl. 31).

CHEMCHE GUL. A secondary *gul* appearing on the carpets and bags of a number of different tribes.

CHUVAL, JUVAL. Wide, deep bags used for transport and storage in the tent, where they are usually suspended from the supporting trellis. Flatweaves are sometimes used for chuvals, but most extant examples are of knotted-pile construction (pls. 2, 3, 20–21, 30, 40–42, 52, 61, 63–64).

COCHINEAL. A red dye from the body of the female insect *Dactylopius coccus cacti* that feeds on different species of cacti, especially the prickly pear. Used since antiquity in Central and South America, the insects were introduced to Europe and Asia only after the discovery of the New World. The dye is highly prized for its rich carmine red and its color fastness.

DARVAZA (DEVERSE) GUL. A large gullike motif used by several Turkmen tribes, most notably the Salor, on trappings in the *kejebe* design (pl. 4).

DYRNAK GÖL/GUL. A hooked-diamond motif used by the Yomut as their main carpet *göl* and as a secondary element by other Turkmen groups (fig. 7 and pls. 28–29, 34, 37).

EAGLE GUL. A misnomer that has now passed into common usage, for the principal motif on three groups of main carpets that differ from each other in certain structural and design features. The term was coined by Bogulyubov, to whom the motif resembled the spread wings of an eagle; the form actually derives from a foliate palmette (fig. 4 and pls. 28–29).

ENSI, ENGSI. Ruglike knotted-pile weavings that are thought to have been used as covers for tent doorways; distinguished by its cross-shaped design format (pls. 7, 17–18, 39, 54, 62).

ERRE GUL. A minor motif on Yomut *chuvals*, *asmalyks*, and in the *alems* of carpets.

ERTMEN GÖL. The *göl* on Chodor main carpets and bags and also on bags woven by the Kizil Ayak and Yomut (fig. 9 and pls. 50, 52).

FLATWEAVE. A term used to describe rugs, bags, and hangings in a variety of weave structures other than knotted pile, including weft-faced plain weave, tapestry weave, and supplementary-weft weaves (pls. 42, 79–80).

GERMECH. A short, wide knotted-pile weaving hung across the doorway of the tent just above the threshold to keep out animals and dirt.

GÖL. According to Moshkova, the primary design motif on main carpets, sometimes regarded as a tribal emblem.

GÜL. (*lit.*, flower) According to Moshkova, the term for the secondary
motif on Turkmen carpets, *güls* are
usually smaller and less complex than
the primary motifs and occupy the in-
terstitial spaces between them. Here,
the term is also applied to primary motifs that lack the emblematic connota-
tions of *göls*.

GUL. The Anglicized version of *göl* and
gül and used as a generic term for
these design elements.

GÜLLI (GUSHLY) GÖL. (*lit.*, *göl* with
flowers, *göl* with birds) Terms used
specifically for the principal motif of
Ersari main carpets, and by extension,
for the similar göls on Salor and
Tekke main carpets and Arabachi
chuvals (fig. 1, pls. 1, 10–13, 16, 55–57,
59).

HERATI. (*lit.*, of Herat) A Beshir carpet
pattern drawn from Persian carpets
of the same name.

IKAT. From the Malay-Indonesian word
for "tie" or "bind." A process, and the
cloth made from it, in which patterning is produced by binding, dyeing, and unbinding the yarns of the
cloth before it is woven; where the
yarn is bound it is not penetrated by
dye and its previous color is retained.
Repeated bindings and dyeings produce more complex patterns and color
combinations. In Central Asia, only
the warp yarns are dyed according to
the ikat process, which produces a
characteristic blurring at color boundaries (fig. 15).

JOLLAR. A term used in Afghanistan
for a wide, shallow bag similar to a
torba.

KAP. A small storage bag (pl. 43).

KAPUNUK, GAPYLYK. (*lit.*, for a door)
A knotted-pile textile, shaped on the
loom to fit around the upper portion
of the tent doorway. It is hung on the
interior of the tent (pls. 24–25).

KEJEBE. A camel litter, covered with
cloth, in which the bride rides in a
wedding procession. In some tribes
kejebe is also used for a design type
special to wedding trappings *(asmalyk)* (pl. 4).

KEPSE (KAPZA) GUL. One of several
main carpet motifs used by the
Yomut (fig. 5 and pl. 33).

KOCHAK, GOCHAK. Motif based on or
named after ram's horns.

KUFIC. An angular, hieratic Arabic
script which gave rise to several rug
motifs usually found in borders.

KURBAGHE GUL. A secondary motif
in some Tekke main carpets and
occasionally on bags woven by
other tribes.

MAFRASH. A small rectangular storage
bag.

MAIN CARPET. The largest of the Turkmen pile rugs, thought by Moshkova
and others to display a motif that
served as an emblem *(göl)* of the tribe
that produced it (pls. 1, 5, 6, 10–13,
28–29, 31–38, 49, 50, 55–59).

MIHRAB. A niche in a mosque that indicates the direction of Mecca and therefore the direction of prayer; a niche-
shaped device on some prayer rugs
that symbolically represents a *mihrab*
(pls. 51, 75).

MINA KHANI. A field pattern found on
Ersari carpets and *chuvals* consisting

Kochak, gochak

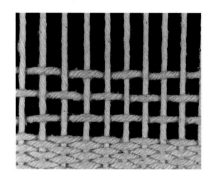

Plain weave (upper section);
warp-faced plain weave
(lower section)

of stylized flowers at the intersections of a diamond lattice; derived from a Persian design type.

NAMAZLYK. A prayer rug often, but not always, decorated with a *mihrab* (pls. 51, 75).

OK BASH. (*lit.,* pole head) A baglike cover placed over the ends of bundled tent poles transported by camels during wedding processions and migrations (pls. 47–48).

OMURGA GÖL. The primary motif on carpets of some Saryk and Ersari groups. Same as *temirjin* (fig. 3 and pls. 5, 58).

PALAS. Large flatwoven rugs with supplementary-weft brocading on a plain-weave ground (pls. 79, 80).

PILE. A surface formed by yarns, cut or in loops, that project from the plane of the foundation fabric. In Central Asian rugs, pile is formed by the cut ends of individually inserted "knots" (see rug knots). Velvet, velour, corduroy, and terry are also pile fabrics but of different construction.

PLAIN WEAVE. The simplest interlacing of warp and weft elements, with each weft unit passing alternately under and over successive units of the warp. Plain weave is said to be *balanced* if the warp and weft are equally spaced and of equal size (upper half of illustration). When the warps are more widely spaced and equal to or finer than the wefts, the wefts are easily compacted and will conceal the warp, producing *weft-faced plain weave* (lower half of illustration).

PLY. To twist together two or more singles (single-ply yarns) to make a heavier, stronger yarn; the number of yarns comprising a plied yarn is written as 2-ply, 3-ply, etc. (see twist).

RUG KNOTS. The principal knots used in Turkmen rugs are symmetrical and assymmetrical.

SAF. A prayer rug with multiple mihrab-shaped niches.

SHED. An opening formed by selectively separating the warp yarns into two planes to allow for the passage of the weft. In plain weave, for example, even numbered warps always form one plane of the open shed and odds the other, reversing positions after each weft passage.

SHOT. One passage of the weft from selvage to selvage.

SINGLE, SINGLE-PLY YARN. The simplest continuous combination of fibers that have been spun to form a usable yarn (see twist).

SUPPLEMENTARY-WEFT BROCADING. A means of patterning a ground fabric (plain weave or weft-faced plain weave in Turkmen textiles) using extra, or supplementary, weft yarns to produce floats on one or both faces of the fabric (pls. 79, 80).

TAUK NUSKA GÖL. A term given to an octagonal *göl* appearing on carpets of the Yomut, Chodor, Arabachi, Kizil Ayak, and Ersari (fig. 2, pls. 35–36, 49, 53, 60, 68, 77–78).

TEMIRJIN GUL. The same as *omurga gul*. The term possibly derives from the Turkmen *demir* (iron) and *-chi* ("one who is occupied with"), thus "ironsmith," a trade associated with settled populations.

TENT BAND. Woven bands in a variety of widths and structures used to stabilize the structure of the tent. Bands decorated with bands, like those shown in this catalogue, serve a decorative purpose (also see *ak yüp*).

Symmetrical knots

Asymmetrical knots, open to the left

Asymmetrical knots, open to the left;
alternate yarns slightly depressed

Symmetrical knots tied on the upper
warps of the open shed

Supplementary-weft brocading

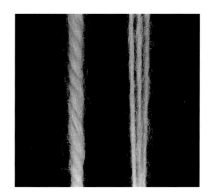

Twist, S and Z

TORBA. A wide, shallow bag used for storage or transport (pls. 8, 23, 65).

TWIST, S AND Z. The direction in which a yarn is spun or plied, which, when the yarn is viewed vertically, corresponds to the diagonal element of the letter S or Z. The illustration shows three Z-spun singles (right) that have been plied to form a 3-ply yarn, plied in the S direction (left). In the weft and pile yarns of many Turkmen weavings, two singles are paired but not plied, which can be represented with the letter "I."

WARP. The longitudinal elements of a fabric that are fixed to the loom and are interworked at right angles by the weft.

WEFT. The transverse elements of a fabric that are usually at right angles to the warp, which interwork with it across the fabric's width.

Produced by the Publications Department of the Fine Arts Museums of San Francisco:
Ann Heath Karlstrom, Director of Publications and Graphic Design; Karen Kevorkian, Managing Editor.
Photography by Don Tuttle Photography, Emeryville, California. Copyediting by Frances Bowles.
Book and cover design by Christine Taylor, Wilsted & Taylor, Oakland, California.
Typeset in Granjon with Nicholas Cochin Black display at Wilsted & Taylor.
Printed by Snoeck-Ducaju & Zoon, Gent.